THE
CHARLESTOWN
CHRONICLES

THE
CHARLESTOWN
CHRONICLES

CATHAL HENRY

First published 2009

Nonsuch Publishing
119 Lower Baggot Street
Dublin 2
Ireland
www.nonsuchireland.com

British Library Cataloguing in Publication Data.
A catalogue record for this book is available from the British Library.

ISBN 978 184588 967 8

Typesetting and origination by The History Press
Printed in Great Britain

CONTENTS

Acknowledgements 7

Preface 8

Foreword 9

About Charlestown 11

Politics 45

Sport 83

Entertainment 101

Memories of Charlestown 127

ACKNOWLEDGEMENTS

I would like to thank the following people for their help and co-operation in the production of this book: my mother Delia and late father Tony, for their patience and articles written; Patsy Dunne MCC, RIP, and Paddy Henry, RIP, for their interest and contributions; Mary Esler and Michael Hambly of Mayo–Ireland Claremorris for their advice and help; Gerry Durkin and Ted McDonnell, and everyone who gave me photographs; Ivor Hamrock, of the local studies section, Mayo County Library, Castlebar, for his valuable help, and last but not least, Nonsuch Publishing for their interest in the project.

PREFACE

To understand the present we need to examine our past. People, places and events through time made us what we are. However, succeeding generations always regret not having engaged more with their elders in exploring and recording the past. Too late we realise what we have lost. For this reason the publication of Cathal Henry's *Charlestown Chronicles* is to be welcomed.

Cathal always had a great interest in fostering the written heritage of his native Charlestown. Through my work in the local studies section of Mayo County Library, over many years, Cathal and I have exchanged a great deal of material on the Charlestown area. He has been generous in donating many rare and historical documents to the library, ensuring their preservation for the future. Cathal's book is also a work of preservation. I know that it will be appreciated and cherished by the present and future generations of Charlestown people.

I congratulate Cathal on the publication of this important work.

Ivor Hamrock
Mayo County Library
Castlebar

FOREWORD

There is a vast amount of historical information available in many areas of Co. Mayo. Much of this information has been put together by amateur historians who have taken on the task of informing themselves on the people, places and events that have shaped those localities that we refer to as our native places.

Charlestown has long been a town of strategic importance to Mayo. It has provided many prominent and dedicated residents who have made their contribution not just to their own areas but to the county at large through involvement in public life, sport, community development and business.

The Henrys have been committed to the growth of the town for generations and have made their mark on politics, commerce and art. They are part of the history of the area.

Cathal Henry's decision to draw together the many articles on Charlestown, its places of interest, its characters, its people, and its changing streetscape and hinterland is another example of unselfish commitment to his home town.

The compilation of this history of Charlestown has been painstaking, the research has been detailed and a fine body of historical data has been prepared. Getting the information together is one thing; having it published is another.

Cathal Henry's decision to go ahead and publish this volume is a brave one and his endeavour deserves to be supported by Charlestown people wherever they may be presently located. For Cathal, the work has been a labour of love and yet another important contribution to Charlestown and to Mayo.

Christy Loftus

'CHARLESTOWN'

Amid the crisp Mayo skies
On a cold December's day
A town still quiet new emerges
There you stand with many facades
Like leaves from a story ready to be told

Dotted on your landscapes are fortresses
Where hunter-gathers came
With herd and kin
Engraving a life that has now since past
Traces of ancient souls
Lie upon the plains of Barnacahogue

In a graveyard at Tample lies the tomb of Costelloe
Dressed by well and relic of St Attracta
The abbey of Urlaur now destroyed
Once echoed with monks at evening prayers
Who chanted songs to a rising sun.

Reminders of history lie hidden within
The very heart of you,
Recollections of times past
Where famine ravaged the limbs of Ireland
And took the salt of mother earth
Tragedy scorned you
Through mines at Maypole
Men of Charlestown lost their lives
Mothers grieved and beat their breasts
For native sons they would see no more

The old town hall stands in glory
Proclaiming a time of finery
Names of Healy and Coogan
Grace its ledges now
Documentation upon shelves of Ash
Tell of your unknown story
While Names of the ascendancy
Pay homage to you
From their resting places
At Tample, Bushfield and Carracastle.

Noirin A. Gannon

ABOUT CHARLESTOWN

COSTELLO

The family Costello are of Cambro(Welsh)-Norman descent, from the family of de Angulo. Gilbert de Angulo, whose surname later became N'angle, participated in the Norman invasion of Ireland (AD 1167-1172) with Richard de Clare (Strongbow).

Gilbert had two sons, Jocelyn and Costilo, and the son of the latter, known as MacOisdeaibh (son of Costilo) participated in the Norman invasion of Connaught in 1235, along with the de Burgos (Burkes) and the de Lacys, and established the Barony of MacOisdeaibh, later MacCostello, in eastern Mayo and western Roscommon, which lasted some four hundred years.

The Costellos were the first of the great Norman families in Ireland to use the 'Mac' (Son of) prefix to their name. Like many other Cambro-Norman families they became 'More Irish than the Irish themselves'. The Barony of MacCostello is still an identifiable geopolitical district in Mayo, and the Costello name is common in the county. Charlestown is very much part of this Barony.

For this information, my thanks to Bob Costello. As an addendum to the Costello saga, the following may be of interest, relative to the place where the Romantic Tomás Láidir Mac Costello was murdered and relayed to me by my mother, Delia Henry. One day in 1934, when teaching in Tavneena National School, the Principal, Mr Gerry Henry asked my mother if she knew where 'Sithestin' west of Swinford was. Although she lived in Killaturley, Swinford was our postal and market town and she went to secondary school there. She had never heard of that place, but said she would find out if it existed. An elderly neighbour, Luke Tunney visited in our house. He was about seventy years of age at the time. On his next visit, my mother put the question to him about the village named Sithestin, west of Swinford. After a few moments, he said, 'No, there is no Sithestin, but Sithestin Dubhaltaigh, now known as Barcul. It is situated between Shammer crossroads and the Charlestown–Ballyhaunis road.' My mother had never heard of the word 'Dubhaltaigh' before, but had cycled through Barcul many times.

The next day she repeated the statement made by Luke Tunney. The Principal got a book called *The Love songs of Connaught* by Douglas Hyde and there in the print was Sisthestin a Dubhaltaigh, Dudley's Sithestin. The poem 'Una Bhain', composed by Tomás Láidir MacCostello, about his lost love, Una McDermott, was on page 117 and underneath it was an account of that place, where he was murdered by the Dillons.

The descendents of the Costellos in the Charlestown area owned around two hundred acres of land at one time, and their tomb is in Tample graveyard, complete with the following inscription:

GLORIA IN EXCELSIS

O Lord have mercy on the soul of Thomas Costello Esq., of Hagfield, who departed this life, February the 1st, 1822, aged 95 years, also his wife, Maria Costello, who departed this life, 6th of January 1810, aged 75 years.
His son Thomas Costello Esq., who departed this life, August 1st, 1828, aged 78 years.
His son Edward Costello Esq., who departed this life, the 2nd of August 1811, aged 59 years.
His son Richard Costello Esq., who departed this life, the 1st of September 1859 aged 95 years, and his grand-daughter Louise Costello, who departed this life, on the 10th of June, 1860, aged 19 years.
Erected by Peter Costello Esq.

The Bridge, Charlestown, taken from the square in the 1930s.

Also buried in this tomb are the following descendents:
Frances Wynne, née Costello, wife of Andrew Wynne.
Margaret Mulligan, née Wynne, who was buried on the 16th of February
1987, by her son James 'Seamus' Mulligan.

The descendents of the Costello family named above still live in the Charlestown area. They include James 'Seamus' Mulligan, his nephew Michael Giblin, and nieces Marcella McBrien, Patricia Leonard (Aclare), Evelyn O'Keefe, and Jacqueline Cummins (Swinford).

Maire McDonnell-Garvey, in her book *Mid-Connacht*, gives a very interesting and detailed account of the Costello era and the transition of their lands to the Dillons. In chapter six, she pays tribute to the great work done by Charles Strickland, Chairman of Gallen and Costello Relief Committee, for the relief of the poor during the Famine years.

Not mentioned in this account, however, is perhaps his greatest achievement – the founding of the town of Charlestown. The first house was built in Charlestown in 1846 and the foundation of the Catholic church was laid a decade later in 1856. The first Mass was celebrated there in 1858. The church and town in the parish of Kilebeagh, in the Barony of Costello, have much to be grateful for the work done by Lord Dillon's agent Charles Strickland.

LOUGHGLYNN HOUSE

Loughglynn House, formerly owned by Lord Dillon, is now owned by the Franciscan missionaries of Mary. Loughglynn is a little lake set in the heart of an ancient forest midway between the towns of Castlerea and Ballaghaderreen in the north of Co. Roscommon. The lands at one time belonged to the Clan Costello, whose main residence was at Castlemore Costello near Ballaghaderreen. Lord Dillon, an Englishman, owned the parish of Loughglynn, three or four parishes in Mayo, Ballyhaunis, Kiltimagh, Charlestown, Tibohine, Fairymount, Ballaghaderreen, Frenchpark, Cloonarrow and Errit. At this time he lived in the old castle at the farmyard in Loughglynn, where the towers stood beside an old church. One of the towers still stands, the other was taken down. It was he who built the house at Loughglynn, as it stands today.

Every Saturday, Mass was celebrated by either the parish priest or the curate. Lord Dillon attended this Mass. Had the British Government known that Lord Dillon was a Roman Catholic, the property would have been taken from him. Eventually this information did leak out and the British Government sent two detectives to investigate. His neighbours told the detectives that they knew of Lord Dillon's presence at Mass because they could hear his footsteps coming into the chapel. However they never saw him there; the reason being that a screen separated Lord Dillon from the people.

The old castle at the farmyard was burned, and while the new house was being built Lord Dillon lived in Dublin, coming now and again to see the work. The out-offices that were left intact were turned into a National School and later into a Cavalry Barracks by the yeomen, Lord Dillon's bodyguards.

One of Lord Dillon's sons married Miss Burke, a Roman Catholic, from Castlemagarrett, three miles outside Claremorris. His father was very displeased with this marriage, and in disgust sold half his property,

Frenchpark. Lord Dillon lived in Loughglynn until his death. He is buried in Ballyhaunis.

The property was given to the next heir, another Lord Dillon, who was not a Catholic. He continued his father's business, taking rents from the tenants. This Lord Dillon had an agent named Whyte, an Englishman. He planted the demense of Loughglynn in the year of the Union, 1801. The demense consisted of all the avenues and stables around the present house. Whyte was an old man, so he shortly retired and returned to England. His successor was Strickland, another Englishman, who made the lake.

Strickland lived in the house at Loughglynn with his wife and family. One of his sons became a priest, Fr William, and celebrated Mass in the old church. The second son, W. Strickland, a sea captain, married a lady who owned a big property in her homeland of Malta. He later became Governor of Malta.

The third son, Thomas Strickland, lived in Castlemore house in Ballaghaderreen. He owned a large Flax Mill in Castlemore. He married a girl from Dublin, and when he retired he went to live there. The fourth son, Charles Strickland, obtained the agency after his father's death. He also married a girl from Dublin, and after his term of office expired, he retired to live in the capital city. He is buried in Glasnevin.

The agency was next taken up by Hussey, an Irishman, whose father was an agent for several landlords in Ireland. He was married to an English girl called Miss Smyth, Daughter of Captain Smyth. He continued the agency until Loughglynn House was burned on 5 November 1896. Hussey had five clerks: Jackson from Birmingham; Thomas O'Connor, later paymaster for the County Development Board, from Dingle; Feeley from Kerry, whose family lived in Ballaghaderreen; Dyar from Roscommon, and Doran, from Tralee, who was a land steward and later became Sir Henry Doran, Head of the County Development Board. Sir Henry lived in Tavrane House, not far from Kilkelly.

Hussey was a kind-hearted man, a great sportsman who loved racehorses and he was liked by all the people. He was manager of all the schools on the Dillon Estate and when he gave them up, the clergy took them over. He lived in Loughglynn until the property was sold in May 1899. He then went back to his father's house in Tralee and his wife went to England.

When the property was sold by Lord Dillon to the County Development Board, the land was divided up among the tenants having small holdings.

The house was repaired by a contractor named Beckett. He demolished one storey and left it as it stands today, with three storeys. His Lordship Most Revd Dr Clancy, Bishop of Elphin, then bought it for the diocese. When the Franciscan Missionaries of Mary came to Ireland in 1903, Dr Clancy offered them the estate as their first convent and it has belonged to the institute since.

A POEM

There is a blue lake far away
Set round with honeyed meads
Where little breezes laugh and play
Among the lisping reeds.
A jewel of a turquoise lake
Blue as a pigeon's wing
Where little waves in music break
And shadowy waters sing.

And in the midst a flowery isle
Enchantment's fairy home,
Where shy wood blossoms sweetly smile
And shy wood creatures roam.
A place to soothe a poet's heart
With balm of leaf and sod
From tumult of the world apart,
A place to dream of God.

The iris lifts a purple plume
In oozy marsh and pool,
The flame-bright marigolds illume
The birchen shadows cool.
The gold bees hum the meadows through,
The darting dragonfly
In brilliant mail of burnished blue
On quazy wings flits by.

The water hen has there her home
Mid lily pads and reeds,
The heron wades the creamy foam
That laps the fringing meads.
The skylark hangs on flickering wing
And pours from heaven his lay,
And finch and linnet flute and sing
For joy the live-long day.
The hazels whisper to the moon,
The birches to the sun,
The flaggers shiver as they croon
Where vagrant breezes run.
The blossom of the sloe is white
And pink the wild rose bloom,
And azure day and purple night
And filled with mild perfume.

There to the fortress of the wave
For peace of soul divine
Fled ancient prince and warrior brave
Of Connaught's kingly line.
From royal court and castle rude
Brehon and bard and chief
Beneath the wood's beatitude
Found refuge and relief.

P.J. Coleman, MA.

THE FIRST HOUSE BUILT IN CHARLESTOWN

In the 1840s, by what is now Charlestown was a bog. Stepping stones across what is today known as the Roundabout (or the Square), led to the ancient town of Bellaghy – where once there was a British Army Barracks – just across the county border in Co. Sligo. There, the Mayo tenants of the Lord Dillon Estate had to carry their sacks of potatoes and grain on market days. Because they were Mayo men and tenants of Lord Dillon, they were forced to wait at the weighing scales until all the Sligo men had their produce weighed.

The Mayo tenants complained bitterly to the agent of Lord Dillon, one Charles Strickland, who protested to the Lord of Sligo estate, one of the Knox family. He was rebuffed, but it was not until later, when Strickland was publicly insulted, that he swore vengeance. 'I will wipe out Bellaghy', he said.

With the consent of Lord Charles Dillon, the 14th Viscount, Strickland immediately offered a large holding of rent-free land forever to the man or woman who would build the first house in what would be a new town. He had takers from many sides.

In the end it boiled down to a two-horse race. The houses were in Main Street (often nowadays referred to as the Square) on opposite sides of the road that comes from Swinford. John Mulligan was the original owner of the site on which the first house was built. His wife was Elizabeth Haran and they had one daughter, Mary. The other site, on which the second house was built, was originally owned by Patrick Egan and then Bridget Mulligan. The two Mulligan families were closely related. Mary Mulligan married Michael Henry from Swinford, and both families lived in the first house that was built. Elizabeth Mulligan died first, Michael Henry in 1862 and John Mulligan in 1876. Mary Henry, wife of Michael, died in 1897. Mary and Michael Henry had two sons; John M., born in 1852, and Mark C., born in 1854.

The race itself is a very interesting story. One July day in 1846, the labourers and builders employed by the Mulligan-Henry family looked across at their opponents and began to worry. Their opponents had now rafters in place and were calling for the slates to finish off the job. Michael Henry decided on a daring move – he would delay the cargo of slates to his opponents. Since Michael Henry hailed from Swinford and had good contacts there, he hurried to Swinford and encouraged a publican there to entertain his opponent's men with their cargo of slates when they arrived. The slates were coming from the port of Ballina. The opponents drank well into the night and were assured that they had won the race. The carter with Henry's slates duly passed through the town and on to Charlestown. The slates were put in place, and the workers laboured all through the night and finished the job.

The first fire was lit and Henrys won the race to build the first house! Henry's opponents, the Mulligan family, were related to Michael Henry's wife, and it is not surprising that relations were a bit cool for many years afterwards.

DISTRESS IN CHARLESTOWN

The following is taken from an 1880 edition of the *Freeman's Journal*:

A crowded meeting was held yesterday, 8 January, in the Charlestown church, for the purpose of forming a sub-committee, for the relief of the poor in this parish.

The following were appointed: Revd T. Loftus, in the Chair; Messrs M.J. Doherty and J. Doherty, secretaries; J. Fitzgerald Esq.; J.W. Mulligan Esq.; J. Morrisroe Esq.; P.W. Mulligan Esq.; J.C. Brady Esq., PLG; M. McDonnell Esq.; P.A. Mulligan Esq.; J. McDermott Esq., Bushfield; J. McDermott, Charlestown; P.J. Doherty; M.J. Doherty Esq., VP, CDS; John Henry Esq.; T. Murphy Esq.; H. Campbell Esq.; M. Moffit Esq.; P.E. Henry Esq.; J. Gallagher Esq.; Patrick Gallagher Esq., PM; J. Cassidy Esq.; Patrick Harrington Esq.; Patrick Mulrooney Esq.; J. Doherty Esq., Tample, and P. Doherty Esq, Tample. The principal male teachers were also present.

The following resolutions were unanimously adopted:

> Proposed by Revd T. Loftus, PP, seconded by J.C. Brady Esq., PLG, that, 'We hereby resolve ourselves into a committee to enable the poor to avail themselves of the funds at the disposal of the Duchess of Marlborough, Mansion House Committee, Dublin.'

> Proposed by J.M. Henry Esq., and seconded by J.C. Brady Esq., that, 'We exert ourselves to the best of our ability, to provide food, fuel and clothing for the starving poor of this parish, in which the destitute families number, to the best of our knowledge, about 700 and to effect this object, that an appeal be made on their behalf, to the Duchess of Marlborough Committee, and the other charitable bodies engaged in collecting funds for the relief of the poor.'

It was also proposed by J.W. Mulligan, and seconded by J. Morrisroe, that the Board of Guardians of the Swinford and Tubbercurry Unions be also involved.

NINETEENTH-CENTURY CLERGY

PARISH PRIESTS

Very Revd Fr Michael Filan, died 1828.
Very Revd Fr William McHugh, served 1828-1848.
Canon James Higgins, 1848-1878.
Canon Thomas Loftus, 1878-1894.
Very Revd Fr Michael Keveney, 1894.

CURATES

Fr Patrick Groarke, 1843.
Fr Michael Muldowney, 1846-1848.
Fr John Gallagher, 1850-1854.
Fr Patrick Davey, 1860.
Fr Paul Henry, 1862-1866 and 1866-1886.
Fr Peter Harte, Fr Michael O'Donnell, Fr John O'Grady, Fr Patrick Hunt,
Fr E. Meehan, Fr M. Cawley, Fr J. Morrin, 1882-1885 and 1885-1894.
John McNicholas and John McDonnell.

The order of churches in Kilbeagh was: Killeen, Tample, Bellaghy and
Charlestown. Fr McHugh lived either in Killeen or in Bellaghy opposite
Mr Moran's Warehouse.

CANON HIGGINS

Canon Higgins, a native of Kilmovee parish and an uncle of Canon Patrick
Higgins, Swinford and Mr L. Higgins, Kilkelly, ministered as Catholic
Curate in Bohola and Ballymote and as administrator in Kilmactigue.

As Parish Priest of Kilbeagh, Canon Higgins lived some twenty years
in Bracklough near the old parish church at Tample. Then as Charlestown
took shape he transferred to a house in the middle of Chapel Street, on the
same side as the church, and he died here in 1878. He built the new, cor-
rectly proportioned Gothic church of Charlestown. In it there is a memorial
tablet to him, and also one for Fr Paul Henry who died here in 1866. There
is also a memorial tablet for Fr John Morrin CC, uncle of Canon Morrin,
Collooney, and brother of Mr James Morrin of Kiltimagh, who donated the

pulpit through Fr Charles Gildea, in memory of Fr Morrin who died in Ballaghaderreen around 1895.

CANON LOFTUS

Canon Loftus, who succeeded Canon Higgins, was a native of Aclare, an uncle of Mr Val Loftus, and a massive, broad-shouldered priest of fine presence and affable manner. He built the Parochial House and later on left it to become parish priest in Ballymote, being succeeded about 1894 by Fr Michael Keveney.

THE FILANS

Concerning the first parish priest of Kilbeagh, Fr Michael Filan, Dr O'Rourke, a painstaking and careful historian tells us that the distinguished Filan family, noted for priests, belonged to Killasser. He makes reference to Fr Michael, PP Kilbeagh, and his younger brother, Fr James, PP Curry. He also refers to Fr Michael Filan and his brother Fr A.D. Filan, who were pastors in Philadelphia, and then commemorates, always in a laudatory way yet another pair, Fr Michael, who went to Mobile diocese, and Fr P.A. Filan, then CC in Gurteen. They were all born in Killasser and all educated in Ballaghaderreen. The Archdeacon rounds off his account of the Filans with a sketch of Fr James Filan, PP Curry, one of the most distinguished priests Achonry ever had.

JAMES FILAN

Of the first batch of students to enter Maynooth in 1795, James Filan read a brilliant course and was appointed on ordination as Professor of Humanities. He relinquished his position after a few years at the request of the Catholics of Sligo town, and in 1807 started and successfully maintained the first Catholic church in Sligo until he was invited back to Achonry, to be parish priest in Curry, and in commendam Adm. in Kilmactigue. Fr James was a ready writer, an educationalist and until that time, the greatest pulpit orator ever heard in Sligo town. He died in 1830 and was buried in Drumahillian graveyard.

I add to Dr O'Rourke's account on the Filans a few more details. They had come from Co. Roscommon, settled in Killasser, and were closely related to Dr McNicholas, Fr James and the future bishop having been professors together in Maynooth. Fathers Michael and Dudley of Philadelphia were nephews of Fr James and uncles of Mrs M.C. Henry, Charlestown, and in turn, nephews of the Philadelphia priests were Fr P.A. Filan (brother of Mrs Henry and uncle of Michael Henry, Jack Henry, Tony Henry and May Henry) and the Fr Michael Filan who went to Mobile. Though the Filans have passed on, the family tree hath still a bloom, their relation and worthy representative being a genial, well-loved priest, Fr Anthony Durcan of Keash.

To come back to Kilbeagh, our subject Fr Michael Filan lived in Marron's in Hagfield and in Harrington's. He died in 1828 and was buried in Tample, where the parish church then was, and his gravestone bears this epitaph:

Gloria in Excelsis Deo.
Here lie the remains of Revd Michael Filan,
who departed this Life on the 7th of January 1828,
aged 42 years.
As he often preached for his flock,
So may they often pray for his soul.
Requiescat in Pace.

Another priest buried in Tample is Fr James Murphy, brother of Mr Thomas Murphy and of Mr Pat Murphy, the Mills, Charlestown, now the home of Miss Berney White. Fr James died as CC in Keash in 1881. There was a Fr Peyton, who was a native of Charlestown, and who lived in Barnacogue. People ascribed thaumaturgy to Fr Groarke. Fr Gallagher (or Fr O'Gal as he was called) was from Killasser and lived in Thomas Harrington's of Bracklough. Fr John McNicholas from Killasser lived in Bellaghy, as did the other curates of the parish.

PASSIONISTS MISSIONS IN CHARLESTOWN IN THE 1870S

The Passionist order gave a mission in Charlestown in May 1874. There were four priests of the Anglo-Hibernian province, and their Irish base

The interior of St James's Catholic church, Charlestown.

was in Mount Argus, Dublin. The priests were Fr Alphonsus, Fr Arthur, Fr Sylvester and Fr Malachy. The mission ended on 24 May with 9,000 communions, and 10,000 people were present at a Papal blessing in the open air. A mission cross was also erected and there were 976 people confirmed by the Bishop.

Fr Alphonsus O'Neill was rector of St Saviour's Retreat, Broadway, Worcestershire, and was second provincial consultor. Fr Arthur Devine was Lector (Professor of Students) in St Anne's Retreat, Sutton Park, St Helen's, Lancashire. Fr Malachy Graham was Professor to the students in Mount Argus. Fr Sylvester McManus was a member of the Mount Argus community.

Fr Arthur Devine later published many books which were widely appreciated, including *The Creed Explained*, *The Commandments Explained*, *A Manual of Ascetical Theology* and *A Manual of Mystical Theology*. Fr O'Neill died in 1899, Fr McManus died in 1902, and Fr Arthur Devine in 1919.

JAMES PARSONS

AN APPRECIATION BY TOMMY O'DONNELL, 8 JANUARY 1955

Mr James Parsons, whose death occurred recently, was the last survivor of a truly remarkable group of patriotic Charlestown men who made their native place one of the most progressive small towns in Ireland. An ardent nationalist and an indefatigable worker, he throughout his long life took a leading part in every effort for the advancement of the welfare of the people.

As a town, Charlestown is young, being little more than one hundred years of age. It was particularly fortunate in the man who built it – Charles Strickland, agent for the Dillon estate. From his foresight came those striking features which impress every visitor – a spacious square and exceptionally wide straight streets. Not so obvious to the stranger however, is the fine system of circular roads by means of which it is possible, on approaching the town by any of the five main roads running through it, to make an exit on any of the other four without passing through any of the streets.

Moreover, Strickland's layout provided for every house (save three or four located on a bend of the Mulaghanoe River) a large backyard and garden plot. One wonders whether a trained planner sitting down today, when there is so much discussion about and so much money spent on town planning, could, given a similar site and similar materials, produce anything better than the Strickland idea. If Charlestown was fortunate in that respect, it was doubly blessed in having, in the 1890s and 1900s, a zealous and enlightened band of residents who rightly considered that amenities that might have been considered adequate in 1846 needed to be supplemented according to twentieth-century requirements, although it was in no means badly off in comparison with conditions in other centres at that time.

There was a plentiful supply of water from an excellent well at the foot of the rising ground in Howley's field, but no dwelling had a piped supply. The first sewers, which were in fact, drains covered in with flagstones, were no longer functioning quite satisfactorily. There was no public lighting; homes depended on paraffin oil lamps. There was no public indoor meeting place, since a great storm had unroofed the old church at Bellaghy, which had been turned into a hall. Fairs were still held in the streets – no great inconvenience, perhaps, at a time when traffic was negligible compared with what

Pictured in Bellaghy
*c.*1930 are John
Owens, Eddie Kilroy,
Francie Kilroy,
Kathleen Kilroy,
Henry Frain, Paddy
Dunne, Luke Kilroy,
and Miss Towey.

it is today, though undesirable from the health point of view.

The then parish priest, Fr (later Canon) Keveney, a saintly man with a burning desire to improve the temporal lot of his flock, sought the aid of Mark Henry, J.P., Co. C. (who in later times was to be for many years a member of the Dáil and for a period 'Father' of the house), Pat Doherty of the Store, Jimmy Morrisroe (whose brother was afterwards to become Bishop of Achonry, and himself destined to serve as TD), and James Parsons. They were men of vision, but above all, intensely practical. Their integrity and ability inspired confidence, loyalty and enthusiastic support. In the course of a few short years, they gave the town almost everything that a modern community could wish for – a gravitation waterworks from sources at Ballyglass, an up-to-date sewerage system, a splendid Town Hall, an electric lighting plant, and a fair green. Strickland had left two short unfinished sections in his scheme of circular roads. Fr Keveney's committee completed them, an undertaking involving the construction of a second bridge over the river. Furthermore, existing footpaths were extended along the roads leading out of the town.

What did these great improvements cost the public purse? It is perhaps difficult to believe today the only permanent charge on the rates amounted to a mere sixpence in the pound, that being the levy in respect of the waterworks and sewerage. The rest of the required expenditure came from voluntary contributions, willingly given because of the magnificent leadership of Fr Keveney and his energetic collaborators, plus some small grants from the Congested Districts Board. These considerable achievements became possible only because five devoted and far-seeing men gave most lavishly of their time, industry and talents to the planning, execution and supervision of the various works. I well

A group of Charlestown citizens in front of St James's church, Charlestown, *c.*1935. Left to right: Luke Mulligan, John Cassidy, Tony Henry, Luke O'Donnell, James Parsons, Luke Colleran, Val Harrison, Mike Brennan, Jim Mulrooney, Billy Campbell and Pat Campbell.

remember that most lovable pastor Fr Keveney being the first person on the job at 7a.m. every morning. Having seen the day's programme well begun he returned to the church to celebrate the early Mass. And in so far as his priestly duties allowed, he went on throughout the day visiting the projects in hand.

His co-operators had large and successful businesses of their own to attend to, yet they always found time to serve in the public interest as well. It is gratifying to observe that the admirable civic spirit which they fostered to so high a degree still flourishes in the parish, as evidenced by the many further improvements carried out in recent years, which are too well known to need to be specified here.

As a young man, James Parsons spent some years at Leith, Edinburgh, in training for the management of the Merchant Tailoring establishment set up by his father, an establishment which, in association with his brother Michael, he continued to run until his retirement a few years ago. On the passing of the Local Government Act of 1898, James Parsons became one of the first members of the Swinford Rural District Council; he was also a member of the Board of Guardians and retained his membership of both bodies for more than twenty years.

Until the new Town Hall was erected, he kept up a custom begun by his father of making their home a meeting place for local clubs and societies. There were stored the drums and fifes, the banners and flags of the Land League and the United Irish League. Away back in 1888, James Parsons was one of the founders of the famous Sarsfield GAA Club, a combination which figured prominently in county and provincial football champion-ships, and which happily is still alive today, with one of the finest Gaelic parks in the provinces. Two of his brothers, Martin and Willie, were playing members of the club. As became a man whose greatest pleasure was serv-ice to his fellows, James Parsons maintained to the last his abiding interest in public affairs. His wise counsel and ready help were always available to anyone in difficulty. His home was ever open to those in doubt or distress and nobody went away without the comfort of his advice and assistance.

May his generous soul rest in peace.

THE TOWN HALL

The Town Hall in Charlestown was built around the year 1900. The Indenture of Lease was made on 10 May 1911, between the Congested Districts Board for Ireland, of 23 Ruthland Square in the City of Dublin, who were the registered owners of the land and known as 'the Board', on one hand, and Patrick Doherty, James Parsons, James Morrisroe and the Revd Michael Keveney PP, all of Charlestown, termed 'the lessees', on the other.

The said gentlemen named above as the lessees, were appointed Trustees for that land, containing three acres and thirty-two perches or thereabouts, with the building thereon. The lease was for a twenty-year period and the

Trustees were charged as from the first day of July 1909, yielding and paying during the said term the yearly rent of £5 by two equal half-yearly payments on the first day of January and the first day of July. The official seal of the Congested Districts Board was affixed in the presence of, and signed by, one J.R. O'Brien, Secretary of the Board.

The Trustees signed the agreement of the lease in the presence of Mark C. Henry, JP, Charlestown. The Trustees of the Town Hall in 1928 were: Most Revd Dr Patrick Morrisroe, Bishop of Achonry; Fr Charles Gildea, PP; James Parsons, and James Morrisroe. In 1938 the Trustees were: Most Revd Dr Patrick Morrisroe; Canon Ambrose Blaine; James Parsons, and Michael O'Rourke. Down through the years various committees of local men were formed, with the approval of the Town Hall Trustees, to look after the welfare and running of the hall, and the varied functions held therein.

VARIETY CONCERTS AND PLAYS IN THE EARLY DAYS OF THE TOWN HALL

A concert and play were staged in the Town Hall on St Stephens's night, 26 December 1905. It may well have been the first such type of entertainment

The Square, Charlestown, in the 1930s.

staged there. The play was *An Doctuir*, which dealt with the dawn of the Irish Language revival. The cast included T.P. Quinn, James Quinn, P.J. Cassidy, Jim Mulrooney, May Henry, and also involved in the presentation were Willie Gallagher, Tommy O'Donnell, Theresa Cassidy and May Stenson.

Those who participated in the accompanying variety concert were Misses Annie McDonnell, Kitty Mulligan, Ethel Doherty, Margaret and Mary Doherty, and P.J. Henry, Michael Hurst of Swinford and a Miss Burke.

During the Civil War of 1921-1922, part of the building was burned down. On being rebuilt it was reopened in 1926, with a dress dance as the first function. Among a variety of events staged or held in the hall, which was a fine spacious building of two storeys, were dances and various indoor sports.

The local drama players, namely the St James Dramatic Society and the Little Theatre Group, by now amalgamated, staged various plays and concerts. Many of the travelling companies trod the boards of the famous building, such as the Dobells, McMasters, McMostins, Carrickfords, Howards, Blacks and Macks, to name but a few.

Film shows were also held there, screened by the Picture Company, Swinford. A room was also set aside for card players and craft classes in crochet and woodwork. Domestic economy classes and Irish language classes were also held and it was the exhibition place for the local agricultural and horticultural shows which were held in the town in the 1940s.

THE POST OFFICE

The British Post Office Archives hold all the records prior to 1921. Charlestown first appeared in the *British Post Office Guide* in January 1869. As it did not appear in the guide of the previous year, it must have been established some time in 1868. The head office at that time was in Swinford. Charlestown first appeared in the *Irish Post Office Guide* in 1922, with Claremorris as head office. From 2 February 1874 onwards the staff at Charlestown sub-post office consisted of a sub-postmaster and four postmen.

CHARLESTOWN SCHOOLS

Lowpark National School, Charlestown, was built in the year 1846, with funds granted by Lord Dillon and the local Board. The roll number was 4794. It was built in the Barony of Costello. There was no rent paid. The precise date of the opening of the school was 2 January 1846. This building is now Murphy's Garage and residence; the new school is directly across the road. The manager of the school in 1846 was Revd Canon Loftus PP.

On the next page is a list of school teachers who resided in Charlestown and taught in the various schools in and around the parish, from approximately 1910:

Charlestown National School, 1948. Back row, left to right: Michael O'Donnell, Peter Frain, Eamonn Walsh, Tommy Jordan, Kieran Grady, Raymond Weaver, Kevin Kilroy, John Mahon. Third row, left to right: Paddy O'Donnell, Charlie Cahill, Paddy Hanratty, Tom O'Connor, Brendan Cafferty, Sean Morris. Second row, left to right: Eugene Owens, Brendan McIntyre, Peter Duffy, Tom Grady, Michael Egan. Front row, left to right: John Jordan, Joe Murtagh, Willie Madden, Kevin Walsh, Justin Honan, Michael McGrath.

CHURCH STREET

Mr & Mrs John E. O'Doherty

Mrs Mary E. Lyons

Mrs Catherine Casey

Mrs Margaret Durcan

Mr Patrick Cassidy and Mrs Mary Kate Cassidy

Miss Margaret Mulligan

Mrs Annie O'Shea

Mr Joseph Campbell & Mrs Tellie Campbell

Mr Matthias Coleman & Mrs Lucy Coleman

Mrs Una Leavy (*née* Brennan)

Mrs Myra Grimes

Sister M. Ursula Reynolds

Sister Aiden Finneran

Sister Thomasina Gilfillan

Sister Brendan Dodd

Sister Mary de Chantail O'Halloran

Sister Marty Richardson

Sister Elsie Gilmartin

BARRACK STREET

Mr Michael Francis Swords & Mrs Mary Swords

Mrs Mary Brennan

Mrs Annie Burke

Mrs Bridgid Parsons

Mr Michael Brennan

MAIN STREET

Mr John Cassidy

Mrs Sarah Dooney

Mrs Annie Campbell

Mrs Delia Henry

Mrs Margaret Swords

Mr John Murphy

Mr Patrick Collins

Charlestown Boys' National School, 1950/51. Back row, left to right: S. Blake, J. Brennan, P. Henry, J. Walsh, J. McLoughlin, V. Owens, J. McIntyre, J. Gallagher, K. Barry. Middle row, left to right: J. Donoghue, T. McGowan, T. Henry, C. Henry, M. Horkan, C. Casey, B. Doherty, S. Foley, J. Horgan. Front row, left to right: D. McIntyre, S. Marren, N. Cassidy, T. Rogers, V. Maloney, J. Casey, F. Henry, S. Walsh, J. McCormack.

Girls' school photo, 1948, including Marie Gallagher, Rosaleen Bermingham, Bridget Mary Brennan, Kathleen Blake, Mary Casey, Carmel O'Donoghue, Margaret Coll, Toinetta Tunney, Finola Bermingham, Patty Brady, Kathleen Egan, Ann Cassidy, Mary Normanly, Mary Brennan, Martina Jordan, Maureen McGowan, Ann Harrison, Bernie White, Patricia Cassidy, Evelyn Henry, Margaret McCormack, Christina Maloney, Ita Carr, Joan Carr, Johanna Kilroy, Teresa McGrath, Peggy Egan, Mary Fitzpatrick, Helen Flood, Dorothy Butler, Attracta Moffitt, Maureen Irwin, Maura Maloney, Lilly Lynch, Imelda Cassidy, and Pauline Mahon.

BALLYGLASS ROAD
Mrs Annie Giblin
Mr Patrick Joseph Merriman
Mrs Breege Gallagher

BELLAGHY
Miss Bridgid Griffin
Mr P. Reid

SECONDARY EDUCATION

There was no secondary school in Charlestown until 1935 when Miss Cahill of Main Street opened her school and employed two other teachers. The school building was situated at the top of Barrack Street, to the rear of the old Town Hall and power station. The building is now owned by Miss Siobhan Byrne.

In 1943, Miss Cahill closed the school and moved to Dublin. Then the Marist sisters, with the approval of the Bishop, bought the property, which consisted of a school and bungalow. On 8 September 1943, the Marist sisters took up residence and were in charge of a recognised school. There were four teachers, three sisters and one lay, and a sister who taught music.

Marist Convent Pioneers, Charlestown, 1957. Back row, left to right: E. Egan, C. Grady, M. Norman, I. Carr, P. Brennan, I. O'Brien, M. Jordan. Middle row, left to right: S. Durkin, H. Tarpey, C. Maloney, E. Horkan, M. Durkin. Front row, left to right: A. Marren, M. Brennan, Fr Smyth, P. Cassidy, E. henry.

The numbers increased and a house was purchased in Church Street that was formerly owned by the late John E. Doherty NT, and is now in the possession of Mrs Kay McIntyre. The sisters moved in on 19 January 1945. The bungalow was then converted into classrooms.

Land was acquired in Lowpark in 1952, and the foundation stone of the new convent was laid on 15 August 1952. It was completed and blessed on 18 June 1953. It became co-educational in 1967.

The first sister to teach in the National School, Sr Tomasina, was appointed on 1 October 1953 in the boys' school. Another sister was appointed to the girls' school in January 1954. A new National School was opened in 1957 and the Schools were amalgamated in October 1970.

Tavneena National School with Principal Delia Henry, 1960s. Back row, left to right: Patricia McLoughlin, Kathleen Fleming, Joan Doherty, Helen Kenny, Marilyn Campbell, Ann McLoughlin, Francis Doherty, Eugene McLaughlin, Michael McLaughlin. Middle row, left to right: Attracta Campbell, Margaret McLoughlin, Lisa Harrington, Breda Harrington, Rosarie Doherty, Mary Holton, Philomena Doherty, Christina McDonnell, Ann Kenny, Josephine Grady, Anna McLoughlin. Front row, left to right: Michael Ruane, Michael Fleming, Noel Kenny.

Delia Henry and her pupils from Tavneena National School, outside Charlestown church after Confirmation in 1967. Girls, left to right: Josephine McDonnell, Mary Holton, Bridie McLoughlin, Anna McLoughlin, Bernie McLoughlin, Paula Campbell, Josephine Grady, Maura Kenny, Margaret McLoughlin, Ann Kenny. Boys, left to right: Michael McLoughlin, Tommy Fleming, Brendan Kenny, Stephen Doherty, Noel Kenny, Michael Fleming, Gerry Higgins.

TAVNEENA

Tavneena, in the parish of Kilebeagh, comes from 'Tawnyinagh' (in Irish, Tamhnach an Fheadha), meaning a cultivated or arable spot in a waste.

In the year 1835, Bridget Gallagher was born in Lurga (or Carrick as it was then called). When I came to Tavneena to teach in the local National School, the family in that house was known as 'Young Tom's' and the grandchildren are there now. Bridget Gallagher attended the hedge school, which was usually held near the crossroads known as the Star, in the upper Tavneena village. The teacher was Thomas Morris, great-grandfather of the late Michael Morris of Tavneena Upper. He was called Cawful Morris, because his mother was Caulfield by name.

Bridget Gallagher married Raftery in 1858. Her marriage was the last to take place in Tample church or Kilebeagh. This was a thatched structure, and bundles of straw were contributed by the people each harvest to keep the thatch renewed. Mick McLoughlin, great-grandfather of Michael, Tavneena, was married the next day in the new church in Charlestown.

Bridget Raftery had a large family. The youngest daughter, Ellen, born in 1877, attended the old school, which was situated partly in Tommy Jordan's field and partly in the present schoolyard. It had an earthen floor and when rain came through the roof, the pupils used tin saucepans to take the water out. When the present school was finished, Ellen was amongst the first pupils to arrive on the day it opened. However they all got stage fright and ran home!

Ellen's first teacher was Luke Lavan from Hagfield. His brother John succeeded him. Patrick O'Grady from Stone Park, Aclare, was the next Principal. The school was then divided and Mrs Moran, who was Kenny from Lurga, was appointed Principal of the girls' school and Patrick O'Grady Principal of the boys'. Mrs Moran had as her assistants Mrs Durcan and Rose Campbell Prendergast. Mrs Parsons (Brett) replaced Mrs Moran and Miss Kenny replaced Rose Campbell. Mrs Dooney, aunt of Bishop Cassidy, replaced Mrs Parsons and Liz Cassidy replaced Miss Kenny. Mrs Henry, mother of Fr Padraic, succeeded Mrs Dooney and Nan Cassidy replaced her sister Liz, who entered the convent.

Patrick O'Grady was appointed to a school in Kilmovee and Luke Jerry Henry, father of Fr Padraic, was appointed Principal of Tavneena. His wife was assistant in the boys' school when he came there. When Mrs Henry was made Principal of the girls' school in 1923, she was replaced by Miss Dunville, after Mrs O'Shea and Miss Mulligan. When Mrs O'Shea was appointed Principal of Barnacogue National School, she was later replaced by me, Delia Henry, and then I went to Cloonlyon National School. When Mr Jerry Henry retired in Tavneena in 1957, I was appointed Principal in the school, where I had begun my career. Miss Murphy replaced me and Mrs Breege Gallagher replaced her.

The information regarding the hedge school and the old school was given to me by the grandchildren of Bridget Gallagher Raftery, namely Mike and Kathleen Holton, then living in Ballyhaunis. The late John Frain of Tavneena Upper, also gave valuable information, which was told to him by his parents. Bridget Raftery died in 1936 at the ripe old age of 101.

Delia Henry

TAMPLE

TAMPLE DURING THE 1800s

This was once the main town of the area, long before Charlestown was established. The name of the parish in which Tample and Charlestown are situated is Kilebeagh. Nearly a thousand people lived there. This town was mainly made up of the families King, Dogherty and Higgin. There was a church and school in Tample and two priests, Fr Garvey who lived in Barlagh and Fr O'Donald, who lived where McDonalds of Tample live now.

John Dogherty's house was the centre of the town. This was also the local Public House and the barns on his land were the shops. The road going along by Dogherty's was a private road and along the side there was a mill. On the other side there was a forge. The main landlords of the area were the Costellos. They lived in almost royal conditions. All of the family are buried in the family tomb in Tample. Over this grave there is a stone table with all their names carved on it and the dates of their deaths. In those days, this graveyard was the only one in the area and bodies were brought from all over to be buried there. There was a very dedicated woman named Mrs King who looked after the graveyard. Each year she cut the grass with a sickle and made hay with it.

Along Tample River there were huge rocks, each one signifying a Station of the Cross. At the end of these was a big boulder in the shape of a chair. This was where St Attracta used to sit, and each year when the Stations of the Cross were being said each person would sit on the stone and say a prayer. The village also became famous for its yearly pattern. First the pattern was held in Hagfield, along the road. The pattern had an annual Mass celebrated at the well and there were also many sporting events. After some years the local people started to have donkey races in John Doghterty's field. Soon all the events were moved to this field. The pattern was usually held on 11 August each year.

From such humble beginnings the pattern became one of the big social occasions of the year. Photographers were sent to film the activities of the events, like the donkey races, horse races, tugs o' war and bike races. These pictures were shown on a big screen set up in a huge tent. Each night many enthusiastic people turned up to see themselves winning or just taking part in an event.

Still to be seen in Tample are some tunnels that were used many years ago by the Vikings. They were brilliantly built in stone. The Vikings used the caves to hide all the valuables that they stole from the native Irish and sometimes to hide there, as the Irish were afraid to go in after them.

Many years ago people came from England to do Ordnance Survey maps of Tample. Some of these maps are still around. The maps were so detailed that they showed everything from the size of a field to that of a house. The English map makers would stand on top of Donoghue's hill and mark everything on to paper. They used very advanced equipment and many local people wondered what these people were doing. Every few hundred yards they left benchmarks in the shape of a crow's foot. On these were marked the height above sea level. For about twenty years afterwards people used these benchmarks. They were needed to aid workmen who were widening the Knock road. These people spent many a long day digging up local fields looking for them. At this time St Attracta's stone chair and the large rocks for the Stations of the Cross were still to be seen, but alas the chair and stones were taken away when the road was widened.

ST ATTRACTA'S SHRINE

Attracta's well or Toberaraght, in Tample, has been venerated by local people for hundreds of years. Who was Attracta? And where did she come from? As we say in Irish, 'Ní feider a rá go cinnte ca rugadh í.' Nobody knows for certain where she was born. Though both the date of Attracta's birth and her parentage are uncertain, historian Thomas Knox, writing on information from the life of St Patrick, says she was a daughter of Cathbad of Gregraide of Lough Techet (Lough Gara) and lived in parts of the fifth and sixth centuries. Attracta left home against her parents' wishes to become a religious and was supposed to have received the veil from St Patrick, who made her Abbess of a convent he founded at Lough Gara, Coolavin. It is possible that Attracta worked for Christianity in Connaught before Brigid arrived on the scene. She founded a convent in Killaraght in Sligo and another in Roscommon. The hospice that she established near Lough Gara endured for one thousand years.

Many stories and legends about Attracta have been handed down through the ages. It is difficult to know which ones are fact and which are fancy. The following one tells of Attracta's encounter with the King of Connaught. The

King carried away some hostages from the area known as Leyney and held them in his strongholds. Soon their friends liberated them, but the King of Connaught and his troops followed them and came upon them at Killaraght, surrounding them on the land side and leaving no room to escape, except through Lough Gara, which was impassable. However, Attracta, who lived in her convent on the shore, came to their rescue by opening a passage for them through the waters of the lough. Immediately, the waters of the lake divided and the people of Leyney marched through to the opposite shore.

In another tale, the same Chief of Leyney and his people, who were harassed by a ferocious wild beast ravaging the country about the Gap in the parish of Kilmactigue in Co. Sligo, requested the help of Attracta to rid the inhabitants of this scourge, which ended in success. One account states that she despatched the animal with her staff, which was similar in appearance to a small crozier. Another version is that the lady killed the monster, half-dragon, half-bear, with her own hands. In Charlestown parish church, to the right of the high altar, a stained-glass window depicts St Attracta with a beast of strange parts and make-up. The church in Kilmactigue is dedicated to St Attracta. She is the Patroness of the Diocese of Achonry and her cult is very strong, especially in the west of Ireland.

The strength of the veneration in which Attracta has been held for fourteen centuries is illustrated by the act of Pope Pius IX in 1829, when he authorised the Mass of St Attracta on her feast day in the Diocese of Achonry. This was the year in which the Catholic Emancipation Act was signed and the event was of great importance throughout the Catholic Church. It was very significant that the Pope chose to honour an Irish saint and indicates the strength of the devotion to St Attracta at that time. Her name became a popular one among Irish girls and there are many lasting memorials to Attracta, even to this day, in place names such as Killaraght and Toberaraght in our own parish of Killbeagh, and also near Tubbercurry. The name Attracta is sometimes shortened to Atty and it is to be hoped that the folklore that has been preserved by our ancestors will be cherished by the present generation for posterity. There can be little doubt that St Attracta, whose name and fame has survived for hundreds of years, was much loved and respected in the Diocese of Achonry. In 1954, the Marian Year, a shrine was erected in Tample, which includes a statue of the saint and a stone etched with the date 1767. The well is preserved by a surrounding wall. From 1954 on, the rosary was recited by a priest at two o'clock on 11 August each year. In 1977 the Tample committee of that time, with the permission of the parish priest Revd Canon Gallagher, invited Most Revd Dr Flynn, Bishop of Achonry, to come and say the first Mass at the shrine on 11 August. Since then Mass has been celebrated at the shrine each year on her feast day.

Written by Delia Henry in 2003. Many thanks also to Paddy Harrington and Eamon Campbell.

KILGANNON'S ALMANAC, 1907

Kilgannon's Almanac of 1907 listed the prominent figures in Charlestown at that time as follows:

CHARLESTOWN CLERGY
Revd Michael Keaveny, PP, Revd Bradley, CC.

TEACHERS
NS Male: Mr O'Doherty.
NS Female: Mrs O'Doherty.

POSTMASTER
P.J. O'Doherty.

POLICE
Acting Sergeant: Flanagan.
Constables: Mulaey, Conway, Duffy, Taimon, Joyce and Faughan.

MERCHANTS AND TRADESMEN
Brennan, M.J., grocer; Campbell, H., grocer; Doherty, J.P., general merchant; Doherty, J.P., grocer; Fitzgerald, Jas, merchant; Gavahan, Denis, select grocer and general provision merchant; Harvison, J.J., general merchant; Hayden, Luke, grocer; Howley, J.J., general merchant; Henry, M.C., general merchant and hotelier; Kennedy, M.I., general merchant; Morrisroe, John, baker and grocer; Moffitt, B., auctioneer; Moffitt, Michael, general merchant; Murray J., grocer; McDonald, M., general merchant; O'Donnell L.J., grocer; Reid, I., grocer.

MAYPOLE PIT DISASTER

It was five o'clock in the afternoon of Tuesday 18 August 1908, when an explosion ripped the heart out of the cannel mine, No.1 Pit, at the Maypole Colliery, Abram, Lancashire, killing seventy-six men.

The disaster shook the Lancashire coalfield, causing a tragedy unprecedented in the Wigan area. For hours after the explosion, yellow smoke poured from the No.1 shaft, a stark aftermath of the horror underground. Seven bodies were recovered quickly, but it was not until November of the following year that most of the remaining victims were brought to the surface.

The last body was not recovered until 1917, nine years after the disaster, which is still talked about by local miners. The recovery of the bodies was delayed because the pit had to be flooded to quell the underground fire that was started by the explosion. An inquest into the deaths of the seventy-six victims (listed below) was opened on 21 August 1908 and concluded on 8 July 1909. The verdict: accidental death.

There were four victims from the Charlestown area, namely Pat Mulligan, J. McGrath, M. Cafferty and E. Cafferty.

The rest of the victims, some of whom were from the west of Ireland, were: J. Bennett, T. McDonald, Pat Cullen, J. Cassidy, T. Gaskell, J. Holcroft, John Hammons, Tom Jennings, T. Cross, T. Kearns, H. Pimblett, M. McGreal, T. Fishwick, P. Duffy, J. Donnelley, M. House, A. Hughes, P. Caulfield, J. Robinson, E. McDonough, [?] McMalloy, Pat Sloyan, J. Burns, J. Crehan, J. Doyle, M. Boyle, S. Evans, T. Murphy, H. Taylor, L. Rushton, T. Lloyd, Pat Carroll, J. Moran, M. Gallagher, Thomas Groarke, T. Donlon, J. Flannery, [?] McGuckian, W. McCabe, J. Taylor, J. Welsh, W. Moore, A. Devaney, W. Monks, A. Henderson, T. Killoran, R. Pimblett, A. Monks, R. Wilding, J. France, T. McEllin, T. Harrison, P. McGowan, E. France, J. Goghegan, J. Walkden, J. Davies, O. Robinson, C. Ford, J. Kirby, J. Pennington, H. Killoran, J. Hodgson, G. Allen, G. Melling, J. Danson, E. Banks, J. Conway, A. Draper, P. Simm and P. Charnock.

The three survivors were Edward Farrell, W.M. Doran and Richard Fairhurst. Patrick Sloyan, also listed as having lost his life in that terrible tragedy, was from Kilgarriff, Charlestown. He was related to the late John Sloyan and also to the Harrington, Bone, Ruane, Mulligan and Gallagher families.

'THE NO CHRISTMAS BOX BRIGADE'

This poem or song was written by the late Michael Colleran's father, around the time of the First World War. It was written about shopkeepers in Charlestown at that time. Michael Colleran was a tailor by profession and lived in Rannarann, near Bushfield, Charlestown.

You people all both great and small,
Come listen to my song,
A verse or two I'll sing to you,
I'll not detain you long.

Concerning the Charlestown shopkeepers,
I hear that it is said,
They have organised a regiment,
Called the No Christmas Box Brigade.

There is Morrisroe and Campbell,
Two foremost generals in the field,
P.A. Mulligan and Gavigan,
That never yet did yield.

There is Moffit and Mark Henry,
That never was afraid,
They are the seven leading generals
In the No Christmas Box Brigade.

These seven leading generals,
I tell you it's no yam,
They have sent to the Red Cross Hospital
Seven thousand jugs of jam.
Their customers would not buy them,
But the nurses at Belgrade
Can thank the Charlestown Officers
Of the No Christmas Box Brigade.

There is Eggler Duffy, Harrison and Hayden too,
Yankie Murray and Whisker Carroll,
I'll plainly tell to you,

ABOUT CHARLESTOWN

John Doherty from Wigan,
Tommy Honan in from Clare,
They are all wearing the khaki jackets
In the No Christmas Box Brigade.

There is John Case, the Yankie Butcher,
He has made a noble stand,
He has organised the butchers all
To march at his command,
He drills them all around the town,
And these are the words he said,
'I will pass them all, both big and small
In the No Christmas Box Brigade.'

There is Mrs Harrington from Chapel Street,
And Mrs Weaver too,
And likewise Mrs Honan and Baker O'Donoghue,
Tom McDermott and Willie Mulligan,
They are taking a noble stand
Of the Chapel Street section of the
No Christmas Box Brigade.

There is Tom Hopkins from Ballagh Street,
As you may understand,
His name will pass down in history
As a thorough gentleman,
He would not join the regiment
He said 'I am so afraid
They won't be able to beat the Germans
In the No Christmas Box Brigade.'

They then marched over to Bellaghy,
It was getting very late,
But the Collerans and their allies
Soon made them to retreat,
You robbed us of our fairs and markets
Now you want to rob us of our trade,
And ye are all a lot of cowards
In the No Christmas Box Brigade.

Now to conclude and finish
I hope I soon get a chance,
To fight a bloody battle
In the sunny lands of France,
When the Germans will see them coming
They will sorely get afraid
Of that regiment from Charlestown
Called the No Christmas Box Brigade.

POLITICS

POOR LAW ADMINISTRATION

In 1735, Bishop G. Berkeley posed the pertinent question of, 'Whether there be upon earth, Christian or Civilised people so beggardly wretched and destitute, as the common Irish?' One hundred years later there was no improvement, as Gustave de Beaumont testifies, 'misery, naked and famishing, that misery which is vagrant, idle and mendicant, covers the entire country. It shows itself everywhere and at every hour of the day – wretched Ireland bursts upon your view everywhere.'

For seventy years the population grew rapidly despite severe famines. Favourable growth factors were good, export prices for food were encouraging, the pattern of early marriages was continuing and ironically the nutritional excellence of the potato sustained the people. Employment was almost non-existent. Only land guaranteed survival, but rapidly repeated sub-division (despite contrary legislation in 1822) was reducing the size of holdings drastically.

Any margin of safety was eroded when 44 per cent of the holdings measured less than three acres and the population density was as high as 416 people per square mile of arable land. Ireland, in those far off days, was a horrible place to live and try to bring up a family. It is a miracle that we survived as a people.

And so in 1838 an 'Act for the more efficient relief of the Destitute Poor in Ireland' was passed by the British Parliament. It enshrined the principle that' local property must support local poverty'. This Poor Law Act divided Ireland into 130 Poor Law Districts or Unions. Each union was to have its workhouse, administered by an elected Board of Guardians and their officials, all accountable to the Commissioners in Dublin. The cost of administration was to be borne by a levied rate on valued property.

The new units did not respect county boundaries and in 1840 Mayo had five unions, which were: Ballinrobe, Castlebar, Ballina, Westport and Swinford. Generally the unions had a radius of twelve miles from a good market town, where the Poor House was built, and they in themselves comprised several electoral divisions.

Swinford Union was formed on 2 April 1840. It had a defined area of 133 acres and a population of 73,529 in its ten electoral areas. The Board of Guardians numbered twenty-eight, with seven resident Justices of the Peace who were ex-officio members. Three meembers were elected from Charlestown, two each from Achonry, Kilmactigue, Swinford, Killasser, Killedan (Kiltimagh), Aughamore, and Kilmovee, and one each from Toomore, Meelick, Bohola and Knock. The Guardians were responsible for fixing a new valuation on every tenement in the union, and this was to be done as cheaply as possible. Detailed directives were supplied to ensure uniformity, consistency and fairness.

Main Street, Charlestown, around eighty years ago.

The valuation process began after March 1841, and was supervised and co-ordinated by Richard Griffith between 1848 and 1864. Griffith's resulting publication forms the core of today's rating system. During this period of time, Charlestown came into being. The town was originally called Newtown Dillon, but the name was later changed to Charlestown in honour of Charles Strickland.

SWINFORD UNION

The following are extracts from minutes of meetings of the Swinford Union, which took care of the area before the foundation of the Mayo County Council.

SWINFORD UNION MEETING, 23 JULY 1878

Guardians present were: Edward C. Kelly, Michael O'Grady, Michael J. Corley, Thomas Mullarkey, William Clarke, Patrick Clarke, Patrick Cunniffe, Patrick Keane, Edward Gallagher, Luke Kearney, Thomas Mulligan and Hugh McNulty. The meeting discussed the parliamentary grant that was to come to the Swinford Union.

MEETING OF THE BOARD OF GUARDIANS IN SWINFORD, 23 SEPTEMBER 1878

Dr O'Grady presented his list of diets for the inmates of the workhouse. They were as follows:

Diet No.1
Liver Diet – Four ounces of bread and three quarters pint of milk daily.

Diet No.2
Breakfast – Four ounces of bread and one pint of milk daily.
Dinner – Four ounces of bread and one pint of milk.
Supper – Four ounces of bread and a half pint of milk.

Diet No.3
Middle Diet
Breakfast – Four ounces of bread and one pint of milk.
Dinner – Six ounces of bread and one pint of milk.
Supper – Four ounces of bread and a half pint of milk.

Charlestown Market Day, c.1880.

MEETING OF COMMITTEE OF MANAGEMENT OF LOWPARK DISPENSARY DISTRICT, 12 MARCH 1881.

Present were J.W. Mulligan, Chairman, M. Moffit and J.C. Brady. It was decided that the relieving officer would attend from 10a.m. to 12noon on dispensary days. It was proposed by J.C. Brady and seconded by J.W. Mulligan.

MEETING, 2 MAY 1881

A letter from Mr Strictland was read, stating that he will meet the Guardians in Charlestown on Saturday the 14th inst. and he will point out to them the site which he proposes to give for a Dispensary and Medical Officer's residence for Lowpark Dispensary District. The Clerk to inform Mr Strictland that the Vice-Guardians will meet him on Saturday the 14th inst., as requested.

LETTER FROM THE WORKHOUSE, SWINFORD, 31 MAY 1881

Gentlemen, I beg to report that the quality of last week's supplies was good. Some milk was returned and showed the cost of the stimulants for the work. The cost of stimulants for the week was £1 8s 4d, and for the corresponding week last year was £1 8s 11d. The children have been taken out for exercise four times during the week and I would respectfully request that some summer bonnets be given to them, as the cost would be very small.

I am, gentlemen, your most obedient servant, P.J. Durkan.

MEETING, 25 OCTOBER 1881

There were several tenders for the erection of a Dispensary and Medical Officer's Residence at Charlestown and also at Foxford. In pursuant of advertisements having been duly considered, the tender of Mr Patrick Harrington of Charlestown for the building of a Medical Officer's Residence and Dispensary at Charlestown for the sum of £750, and also the building of same in Foxford for £800, was accepted. The buildings at Foxford to be handed over completely furnished in every respect on or before 24 June 1882, and those at Charlestown on or before 24 July 1882. Bonds to be perfected within one week.

Tenders for building an additional apartment for the workhouse porter having been considered, John Mulligan was declared the contractor for the sum of £18, the work to be completed by 1 May 1882.

The proposal of Mr Pat Conwell to make a new horse cart and crib for the sum of £8 was accepted, and to be furnished on 1 January 1882.

MEETING, APRIL 1882

The election of the Chairman for the coming year took place. Mr Cassidy proposed and Mr Moffatt seconded it, that Mr Charles Strickland be elected Chairman for the coming year. Mr Murtagh proposed and Mr Staunton seconded it, that Mr Myles H. Jordan be elected. The voting was as follows. For Strickland: Messrs Mulligan, J. McDermott, Cassidy, Moffatt, Brady and Mellet. For Jordan: Messrs Clarke, William Clarke, Staunton, Murtagh, O'Donnell and Keane. Total votes for each candidate: six. Mr Standish O'Grady McDermott declined to vote. No Chairman elected at that meeting.

MEETING, 18 JANUARY 1884

In relation to the granting of licences for markets in the Swinford Union, the following was received from the Clerk to the Board, 'His Excellency has been pleased to grant a Licence for the holding of a usual weekly Market at Charlestown on the 16th inst. and the usual weekly Market at Kiltimagh on the 17th.'

MEETING, SEPTEMBER 1884

It was resolved that the Board approve the proposal of a line of railway from Claremorris to Collooney.

MEETING, JUNE 1882

Mr P. Harrington [the builder who built the Dispensary in Charlestown] requested a cheque on the 20 June for £200 to pay for slates, and he also requested that a Clerk of Works be appointed to the job.

Several tenders for workhouse supplies having been considered and samples inspected, the following contracts were declared for twelve months:

Best white bread: 5¾d per four-pound loaf, Mr E. Dolphin.
Oatmeal: £11 10s per ton, Mr E. Dolphin.
Calico: 4d per yard, Mr Joseph Erskine.
Irish Linen: 6d per yard, Mr Corley.
Bengal strip: 6¾d per yard, Mr J. Corley.
Flannal: 1s ½d per yard: Mr J. Corley.
Linsley Woolsley: 11¾d per yard: Mr J. Corley.
Blankets: 2s 1d, Ballina Woolen Mills; 1s 9d, Mr J. Corley.
Red rugs, woollen: 5s each, Mr Joseph Erskine.
Shawls, large: 3s 6d each, Mr J. Erskine.
Thread: 2s 6d per pound, Mr P. Manning.
Tea: 1s 6d per pound, Mr R. Woodlay.

MEETING, 22 JUNE 1885

Proposed by Mr Mellett, seconded by Mr Murtagh, that we beg to tender to our Deputy Vice-Chairman our sincere expression of sympathy on the death of his much lamented and esteemed wife, and beg to express to Mr J.W. Mulligan our feelings of sorrow and regret on this event.

Also resolved: that William Lynam, County Surveyor, be requested to furnish to the Board with plans and specifications of the repairs necessary to the public well at Charlestown, with as little delay as possible. [The well is still there at the end of the Well Road, near the graveyard.]

MEETING, AUGUST 1885

Resolved: that the tender of Mr John Doherty, Tample, for the erection of a boundary wall around the Kilebeagh burial ground, at £2 11s per Irish Perch and according to specifications, be accepted.

Resolved: that the tender of Mr John M. Henry, to construct the new sewer at £3 per perch, and according to specifications, be accepted.

MEETING, 20 JANUARY 1891

Proposed by M.C. Henry and seconded by Mr Mulligan that, owing to the distress condition of Sonnagh and Doocastle, which are within the Union and completely deprived of any relief in the shape of work from the Coolooney and Claremorris Railway Line, we are unanimous in directing the attention of the Government to the serious consequences that are likely to arise unless relief works are immediately offered.

The following letter was read to the meeting:

> There are upwards of three hundred families in the Parish of Kilbeagh and outside the reach of railway works, and at present in a state of abject poverty, and as these poor people can be profitably employed in their own neighbourhood in repairing roads, cutting hills, sinking rivers, etc., we recommend these poor people to the consideration of the Local Government Board and hope they will urge upon the Government the necessity of helping these people by giving grants in the above named works.

> The villages of Gleann, Tavneena, Lurga, Kilgarriff, Barnalyra, Barnacogue and Killaturley are the places named as being outside existing railway works and where works of some kind are absolutely necessary to save the people from starvation.

> Signed,
> Thomas Canon Loftus, PP
> J.C. McDonnell, CC

MEETING, 7 AUGUST 1894

Resolved: that Sr Mary Xavier Henry be appointed nurse of the Fever Hospital, Swinford, at a salary of £25 pounds per year, with apartment, fuel and light.

MEETING, 1 OCTOBER 1895

Proposed by Mr Staunton and seconded by Mr Sheridan, resolved: that as this is the opening day of the Coolooney–Claremorris railway line, we adjourn the remaining business of the Board to give an opportunity to the Guardians and others concerned to travel over a portion of the line and see for themselves how they appreciate its completion.

MEETING, 11 JANUARY 1896

Present were: M.C. Henry, Chairman; Thomas Roughneen; J. Devitt; A.J. Staunton; J.J. Durkin; M. Sheridan; Thomas Dunleavy; J. Irwin; Peter Gallagher; Patrick Gallagher, and Thomas Higgins.

The Rate Collector for the Charlestown area at this time was Bernard Moffat.

MEETING, 3 AUGUST 1897

Proposed by Mr Devitt and seconded by Mr Gallagher, resolved: that we have learned with very deep regret of the death of Mrs Mary Henry, Charlestown, mother of our Chairman, M.C. Henry. We desire to convey to him and his family the expression of our sincere sympathy and condolence. We will now adjourn this meeting as a final tribute of respect without transacting any further business.

SWINFORD UNION ELECTION RESULTS, 1902

This account gives the candidates and the districts for which they were elected, as well as the number of votes cast for each:

Aughamore: Patrick Glavey, 88. Thomas Glavey, 88. Timothy Kenny, 73.

Bohola: Patrick Sheridan, 86. Patrick Byrne, 34. John Mulroy, 6.

Doocastle: Patrick Doohan, 73. Edward Geever, 58. John McDonnell, 32. Mr Roddy, 21. Thomas Hunt, 4.

Kilkelly: T.M. Harrison, 210. Thomas Costello, 148. Thomas Kenny, 62.

Kilmovee: M.J. Duffy, 178. J. Irwin, 156. Thomas Fleming, 147.

Sonnagh: M.C. Henry, 270. J. Keane, 224. T. Rush, 77.

Tumgesh: M. Dunleavy, 115. P. Gallagher, 79. P. Peyton, 71.

Swinford: J.A. McNicholas, 250. M.F. Campbell, 248. J. Davitt, 117. P.M. Henry, 8. M. McGough, 4. E. Mulloy, 2.

MEETING, 10 APRIL 1917

In the Chair: J. Marren, JP. Other Guardians present were: E.H. Dolphin, M.C. Henry, J. Mulligan, J.A. Mellett, M.F. Campbell, J. McHugh, T. Marren, P. Deacy, J. Morrisroe, M. Dunleavy, J. Gallagher and M. Murphy.

In the year 1916-1917 Mr J. Garvey of Sonnagh was the Relieving Officer for the Charlestown area.

Photograph taken outside Henry's in Charlestown in 1911 on the occasion of the ordination of Bishop Morrisroe as Bishop of Achonry. Bishop Morrisroe was born in the town.

MEETING, 8 SEPTEMBER 1917

At the meeting Mr John Comer, Swinford, stated that he was directed by Swinford Sinn Féin to forward a resolution and to request that the matter be placed before the Board of Guardians at their next meeting.

The resolution referred to was, 'We call upon the Guardians of the Swinford Union to expunge from the minutes, the resolution of 9 May 1916, condemning the action of the brave men who took part in the Rebellion of Easter week.'

They, Sinn Féin, could not understand how any body of Irishmen calling themselves Nationalists could condemn their countrymen who gave up their lives for Irish freedom.

The resolution was proposed by the Chairman, Mr Campbell, and seconded by Mr P. O'Hara. It was then put to the meeting and passed. The following note was written across the resolution of 9 May 1916, 'Expunge from Minute book.'

MEETING OF GUARDIANS, 25 SEPTEMBER 1917

In the Chair: J Marren, JP. Other Guardians present were: T. Kearney; J. Parsons; J.A. Mulligan; J. Reid, Cloonamna; E. Geever; M.C. Henry; J.P. McDonnell; D. Grogan; P.J. O'Brien; F. Davey; P. O'Hara; R. Barrett; F. Brennan; M.F. Campbell; T. Rogers; R. Folliard; T. Waldron; D.J. Murtagh; E.P. Irwin; T.F. Keane, and M. Murphy.

At this meeting the tender of Mr Michael Mulligan of Swinford for the supply of the following articles of clothing was accepted:

Linen sheeting per yard: 3s 6d
Shirts for men, each: 3s 3d
Flannelette per yard: 10d
Irish tweed per yard: 3s 6d
Corduroy per yard: 2s 6d
Saddler's thread per pound: 6d
Men's caps, each: 1s
Boys' caps, each: 10d

Mr James Dolphin's tender for bread at 9½d per four-pound loaf was accepted. Mrs Mary McNicholas's tender for the supply of milk at 1s 8d per gallon was accepted.

MEETING, 9 OCTOBER 1917

Gentlemen, I have sold two of the workhouse pigs for £23. I purchased three store pigs at a cost of £14 5s. I have lodged to the credit of the Union the following:

Sale of pigs: £22 18s
Balance of cheque from purchase of pigs: £14 6d
Payment of relief: £20 3s 3d
Total: £43 15s 9d

Your obedient servant,
O. McNicholas.

MEETING, 11 JUNE 1918

Proposed by the Chairman P. O'Hara and seconded by Mr Campbell: that we protest against the action of the English Government in the imprisoning and deporting of Irish men and Irish women without giving them a fair and public trial. We demand in the interest of humanity, that Irish prisoners be treated in a humane manner and that a representation of a Neutral Nation be requested to visit the Prisoners and report of their treatment in English prison cells, and demand their release or be given a fair trial before a jury of their countrymen. In the meantime, to see that the prisoners get the privilege of communicating with their friends.

The spring well in Charlestown.

We think it a public scandal that a country which professes to be the saviour of small nations, should at this stage of the war, confine and persecute for no cause but for loving their country.

DISPENSARY DISTRICT

These accounts are taken from the minute book of the Charlestown Dispensary District (1852-1894), which was once in the possession of my late father, Tony Henry, who gave the book to a reporter with the *Western People* and never got it back. The following material then appeared in the *Western People* during the 1940s.

The minute book opens with an account of the first meeting of the committee of management, on 9 March 1852. Present at the meeting were Charles Strickland, Pat J. Mulligan and Dillon Cassidy. The first named was chosen as Chairman, Frances R. O'Grady as Vice-Chairman, Pat J. Mulligan as Secretary, and Dillon Cassidy as Assistant Secretary.

The meetings of the committee were fixed for the first and third Saturdays in each month at 10a.m. Dr P.C. Phillips was appointed medical officer of the district at a salary fixed by the Board of Guardians, and he was directed to make out a list of all medical appliances and medicines that might be required.

The house of Thomas Mulligan was ordered to be taken as a dispensary at the yearly rent of £10 10s. At the next meeting on 20 March, there were present: Pat J. Mulligan, Dillon Cassidy, and Peter Costello. Mr Cassidy was Chairman.

The following list of members of the committee of management was inserted in the minutes: Joseph M. McDonnell, Doocastle; Lord Viscount Dillon, Loughlynn House; Charles Strickland; Francis R. O'Grady, Tavrane; Denis O'Connor, Mount Druid; John Knox, Castlereagh; Richard O'Grady, Carrowbeg; P.J. Mulligan, Lowpark; Dillon Cassidy; Thomas Phillips, Cloonmore, and Peter Costello, Hagfield. The relieving officer was Pat McDermott, Bushfield. The electoral divisions comprising the dispensary district were: Sonnagh, Kilbeagh, Cloonmore and Doocastle.

At the meeting on 17 April, the Poor Law Commissioners wrote expressing approval of the appointment of Dr Phillips, at a salary of £50 per annum. Dr Phillips was still medical officer of the district in 1877. In August 1852, the Poor Law Commissioners wrote complaining of the irregularity of meetings of the committee, and the reply given was that although they had often met, their meetings had not been minuted, but the committee were strictly diligent in examining the register. Thereafter, up to November 1858, the minutes of the monthly meetings of the committee are concerned almost entirely with noting that the medical register had been examined.

In April 1859, the committee resolved that in consequence of the non-attendance at the meetings of Revds Higgins and Devine and Peter Costello, that three other persons should be appointed in their stead and that the members be requested to attend the next ordinary meeting, with a view to dividing the district into vaccination districts. At the next meeting the Commissioners sanctioned vaccination districts as per the following: Doocastle electoral division, Carracastle for Cloonmore ED, and at the dispensary in Charlestown for Kilbeagh and Sonnaugh.

On 23 July 1867, at an extraordinary meeting of the committee, convened by circular with the Revd James Higgins in the Chair, it was resolved that the salary of the medical officer, Dr Phillips, be increased from £75 to £100 per annum, in conformity with the increase given to other medical officers in this Union. Mr Charles Strickland had been elected Chairman each year up to 1868, though he did not appear to attend. He was succeeded in this year by Joseph M. McDonnell, Doocastle, with Dominick D'Arcy as Vice-Chairman, but the Chairman of the meetings thereafter was either James Howley or D. D'Arcy. Mr McDonnell died in 1872 and in June of that year Mr D'Arcy was appointed as Chairman. Mr Luke Colleran was presiding Chairman at the meeting in September 1874, when the rent of Lowpark Dispensary was raised from £10 to £13, in conformity with the increase given for other dispensaries in the Union.

At the meeting of 13 August 1875, it was resolved that, 'Dr Phillips, medical officer, Lowpark District, applied for fourteen days leave of absence, and it being the first time he has ever asked leave of absence during the last twenty-three years we have pleasure in according him the leave asked.' In August 1876, Revd James Canon Higgins was elected Chairman of the committee. No minutes were recorded after that until 16 June 1877, when Canon Higgins was re-elected Chairman.

DR PHILLIPS AND DR STRITCH

In August 1880 the committee met and present were: D. D'Arcy, Chairman, Michael Moffitt and James C. Brady. They had before them a letter from Capt. Spait, the LG Inspector, calling on the committee to consider the advisability of asking Dr Phillips to resign, as he was then a very old gentleman and a long time in the service. The minute book reads:

> Dr Phillips has sent in his resignation and the committee are of the opinion that Dr Phillips is entitled to the highest possible pension after his long service of twenty and a half years. Secretary to advertise for a Medical Officer to take charge of the Dispensary from the first of October 1880.

The committee met on 31 August 1880 and declared they were of the opinion that the salary for a medical officer should be £120 a year, besides all other usual fees. The committee were also of the opinion that the medical officer should reside in or about Charlestown.

On 1 October 1880, the committee had before them applications for the position from Dr Michael Hillary, Dr George A. Stritch and Dr Hubert Flanagan. Dr Stritch was appointed by a majority and Dr Phillips was to get £2 a week while acting for his successor. Dr Stritch took up duty and in December 1880 laid before the committee a red ticket, which he was of the opinion that the recipient was not entitled to, as he had several head of cattle. The ticket was cancelled. The committee considered the question of building a Dispensary house for the Doctor, as there was no suitable residence in Charlestown. Consideration was adjourned.

In August 1881, the committee expressed the opinion that a dispensary house should be built but not to exceed £900, with the doctor paying 3 per cent of the outlay. There was apparently some friction, for on 24 June 1882, the LG Board wrote regarding a complaint made by Dr Stritch in the matter of a charge made by John W. Mulligan at the previous meeting, and the committee expressed the opinion that the matter be allowed to drop.

In September 1882 the committee considered that a new cemetery was required to meet the wants of the locality. In October the committee decided that, 'considering that fever has existed in Charlestown for some time past, owing to the imperfect sanitary arrangements, the Board of Guardians should have an estimate of the cost of a scheme, a loan to be obtained, repayable in fifty years'. In the same month the committee accepted a proposal of Peter Doherty, to give an Irish acre of his land for a graveyard in Lowpark for £30.

'Regarding the charge against Dr Stritch by Mr P.J. Durkan', says a minute of July 1883, 'we are of the opinion that there should be a sworn investigation.' Friction appeared to be growing, for in April 1884, the committee considered that a sworn investigation should be held into charges brought by John McDermott against Dr Stritch. In July of the same year the committee had before them the Inspector's report of the investigation of a negligence charge against Dr Stritch and considered Dr Stritch's attention most objectionable, more especially on account of the poverty of the patients and now ask Dr Stritch to resign.

COMMITTEE MEETING, 28 MARCH 1884

On this date, the members present were: J.W. Mulligan in the Chair, Michael Moffitt, John M. Henry, James C. Brady, and P.A. Mulligan. It was resolved to recommend new sewers to be made from Carbury Egan's to John Duffy's, from John Brennan's to Thomas Regan's, and on both sides of Chapel Street. The LG Board wrote that their medical inspector having admonished Dr Stritch, they were not prepared to require his resignation.

The Chairman reported in November 1884 that he had taken over possession from the clerk of works of the dispensary buildings.

About this time there was a change in the constitution of the committee, for we find that at a meeting of 15 May 1885, Mr Joseph M. D'Arcy was reappointed Chairman, Mr J. W. Mulligan became Vice-Chairman, Mr J. C. Brady was appointed Secretary, and Mr Michael Fitzgerald, Assistant Secretary.

KILBEAGH BURIAL GROUND

A sum of £20 was voted to James King at a meeting on 29 May 1885, as compensation for his interest in the plot of ground which it was proposed to add to the Kilbeagh Burial Ground. The Board of Guardians were requested to have the additional plot of ground properly walled in and the old boundary walls repaired. The committee also recommended that a wall and gate be placed in front of the dispensary buildings according to Mr Hogan's plan.

Was another tiff the explanation for the following entry on 29 May? 'The committee have sent to the medical officer to produce his books, and have received a reply that his books cannot be produced.' A minute calling on the doctor for an explanation was also made. The doctor refused to pay any portion of the expenses of building a boundary wall around the dispensary residence, and it was resolved not to build one. It was urged that the Board of Guardians should carry out a water supply for Charlestown in accordance with the plans of Mr Lynam CE.

DISPENSARY HOUSE

The dispensary residence, then as now, often caused trouble. Dr Stritch, it would appear, complained to the LG Board of the state of the new building and the delay in completing it. The committee repudiated responsibility, stating that the doctor refused to assist the committee in any way in the matter, and asked that the Guardians have the boundary wall and entrance to the buildings completed, so that the LG Board could insist on Dr Stritch taking possession within two months from 3 October 1885.

A special meeting was called arising out of a letter from Canon Loftus regarding fever in the parish. Dr Stritch objected to remaining until the

Canon's letter was read, and an urgent appeal was sent to the LG department, to send medical assistance at once. At a meeting of 26 February 1886, a minute was made that copies of the charges made against Dr Stritch for his refusal to attend should be sent to the Guardians.

All was not as harmonious as it might be in Charlestown, for on 30 April 1886, the following minute was recorded, 'Letter receive from LG Board referring to meeting of committee, which Mr P.A. Mulligan wrote about, we respectfully request the LG Board not to take any further notice of letters regarding the committee from him.' On 18 June 1887 Mr James Fitzgerald was elected Chairman, Mr Moffitt Vice-Chairman, Mr J.C. Brady Secretary, and Mr John M. Henry Assistant Secretary. In May 1888 they were re-elected.

'OMADAWNS AND CODS'

On 29 June 1888, trouble arose, as we can see from the minute:

> Proposed by J.W. Mulligan and seconded by the Chairman, that owing to Dr Stritch refusing to leave the room, the meeting be adjourned to the Courthouse, also owing to Dr Stritch making use of the observations 'Omadawns and Cods', to the members of the committee. At the adjourned meeting in the Courthouse, a resolution was passed urging the LG Board to grant an enquiry into the matter at once, and see if we as members of the committee are to be insulted and disrespectfully treated in this manner by a paid official.

Another resolution was also passed:

> Owing to Dr Stritch refusing to take dispensary tickets and not attending to the poor on three previous dispensary days, we call for an enquiry on the whole matter, and we respectfully ask the LGB to send down a doctor to take charge of the sick and the poor of the district until such enquiry be gone into.

Matters came to a head a month later, when the committee met and read a letter from the LG Board ordering the committee to meet, for the purpose of calling on Dr Stritch to resign his position a medical officer.

The minute of the last meeting continued: Dr Stritch, having heard the above letter read, and being asked by the Chairman to give a reply, refused to resign. At a meeting of 30 July 1888, the committee accepted his resignation. Dr McDermott of Ballaghaderreen was appointed *locum tenens*.

On 31 August 1888, Dr M.A. Brennan was appointed by a majority, the other applicants being Dr James Gunning and Dr Stritch. Dr Brennan got four votes, from the Chairman and Messrs P.A. Mulligan, J.M. D'Arcy, and James Fitzgerald. For Dr Gunning, votes were given by Messrs Thomas Moffitt, J.W. Mulligan and M. Moffitt.

On 25 April 1890, Mr Mark C. Henry is first mentioned as a member of the committee. He became Secretary of the committee on 24 April 1891 by a majority vote, but he appears to have relinquished the job, for in May 1892 Mr Michael Moffitt was appointed. Mr Martin D'Arcy became Chairman and Mr P.A. Mulligan, Vice-Chairman.

The rent of the dispensary house was to be £25 a year, free of rates. On 28 April 1893, Mr M.C. Henry was elected Chairman and Hon. Secretary. In April 1894, Mr J.W. Mulligan became Chairman, with Mr Michael Moffitt as Vice-Chairman and Mr M.C. Henry, Hon. Secretary.

The minutes for the succeeding years up to 1898 were concerned largely with granting leave of absences to Dr Brennan. Then, at the end of the minutes, comes the Local Government Act. The last entry is signed by M.C. Henry, Hon. Secretary. Henry died in 1952 aged ninety-eight years of age.

Bellaghy, Charlestown, Co. Mayo, pictured in the 1930s.

Charlestown Dispensary Doctors from 1846 to 2001 were: Dr Phillips; Dr Strich; Dr McDermott; Dr Carmody, Dublin; Dr Murray, Dublin; Dr Sweeney, Ballina; Dr O'Sullivan, who was married to Willie Doherty's sister; Dr Ahern; Dr Rowland, Crossmolina; Dr Mulligan, Charlestown; Dr Noble, a lady doctor from Dublin; Dr Byrne, Ballaghaderreen; Dr P. Carney, Swinford; Dr Gleeson, Cork, and Dr Martin O'Brien from Headford, Co. Galway.

CONOR O'KELLY, MP

Conor O'Kelly was convicted of breaking the Coercion Act in Co. Mayo and sentenced to two months in prison. The following is the address of welcome by M.C. Henry, Chairman of the Swinford District Council, O'Kelly's release from prison on 22 February 1902:

> On behalf of the Swinford Rural District Council, we offer you a cordial welcome on the termination of the sentence of imprisonment imposed on you by two Removable Magistrates at the instigation of those foreigners who misgovern this Country from Dublin Castle.
>
> The determination to convict you, no matter on what evidence, is best shown by the refusal of the Court selected, to even state a case in circumstances in which the first living Irish lawyer has held you were convicted illegally.
>
> We assure you that our Council joins most heartily in the feeling of widespread rejoicing which today prevails amongst your National fellow countrymen, to know that your services will once more be given to the cause which your untiring and self sacrificing exertions and your eloquent advocacy have done so much to advance.
>
> We sincerely hope that no injury to your health has followed your long incarceration, and we earnestly trust that the gruesome memories of Mr Wyndham's plank bed will be soon effaced by the associations of your old friends and the many enduring ties of attachment which your enforced absence has only bound more closely.
>
> Your imprisonment under the Coercion Act has once again drawn public attention to the hateful tyranny which goes under the name of Government of Ireland. In a country supposed to be free, you have been prosecuted for vindicating the right of free speech and after being given a mock trial at the hands of a Tribunal, selected and paid by your Prosecutors, you have been

sentenced to imprisonment for two months in a British Bastille.

The people amongst whom you live have conferred on you the highest honour at their disposal by electing you to represent them in Parliament, and the people's representatives have on three successive occasions unanimously chosen you as Chairman of the chief governing body of the county. What a strange commentary on the much vaunted 'blessings of British Rule'.

Is the action of a Government which, in prosecuting a representative so honoured and esteemed, not only abrogates the common law of trial by Jury, but sets up its own Tribunal to pronounce judgement? Such mockery of justice constitutes in our opinion one of the grossest scandals that ever tarnished the administration of law in a free country.

We wish to take this opportunity of expressing our grateful appreciation of the splendid services which you have rendered to the National cause. We have observed with the warmest admiration and most cordial approval the manly stand you have made on behalf of the tenant farmers of this country and the earnest and sustained support which you have given to the efforts to affect a remedy for the miseries which result from a dual ownership in the land. We are confident that the imprisonment of you and your colleagues will materially tend to force the demand for legal facilities for compulsory purchase to a speedy settlement, and notwithstanding the prophetic 'never' of a flippant Chief Secretary, we are convinced that the time is now near at hand when the rule of the Rack Renter and the Bum-Bailiff will disappear forever, and when the 'Tillers of the soil' will settle down in peace and contentment to enjoy the rights which have been so long usurped by others.

Assuring you of our highest esteem we beg to subscribe ourselves on behalf of the Swinford Rural District Council. M.C. Henry, Chairman. John Davitt, Vice-Chairman. Joseph A. Mellett. Peter Langley. Thomas Roughneen.

This address was published in the Western People, and as a result an exchange of letters began between M.C. Henry and the office of the Lord Chancellor, who was most displeased at this show of support:

Lord Chancellor's Secretary's Office,
Four Courts,
Dublin,
26 February 1902.

To: M.C. Henry, Esq., JP, Swinford.

Sir,

I am directed by the Lord Chancellor, to say that his attention has been called to the report of the proceedings in the *Western People* of February 22nd on the occasion of the release of Mr Conor O'Kelly, MP, from Castlebar Prison on the termination of his sentence for Unlawful Assembly. You are reported to have taken an active and prominent part in those proceedings, notwithstanding your position as a Magistrate, to have held up Mr O'Kelly's conduct on the occasion for which he was sentenced, as worthy of admiration and imitation.

Such action on your part is entirely inconsistent with your position as a Magistrate and I am directed to inform you, that, if you desire to submit any observation in reference to the foregoing, they should reach me for submission to the Lord Chancellor on or before this day week.

I am to add that His Lordship requires that, pending his decision, you will abstain from sitting on the Petty Sessions Bench.

I am, Sir,
Your obedient servant,
J. Nugent Liutaigne.

M.C. Henry's reply read as follows:

Charlestown
Co. Mayo,
4 March 1902

Sir,

In reference to your letter of the 26th. Concerning my actions on the occasion of the release of Mr Conor O'Kelly, MP, from Castlebar Prison, I have to say: Mr Conor O'Kelly is a personal friend of mine, and as such I thought I was warranted in what I did.

Even now I cannot see that anything I did was inconsistent with my position as a Magistrate, considering Chief Baron Pallai's opinions of the Law in this case.

I am, Sir,
Your obedient servant,
Mark C. Henry.

The Lord Chancellor, somewhat taken aback by Henry's response, was prepared to reconcile the matter:

25th Day of March 1902.

Sir,

I am directed by the Lord Chancellor to inform you that he has considered your reply to my letter (written by direction of His Lordship) drawing your attention to the fact that your attendance at the demonstration referred to was calculated to hold up conduct in respect of which a sentence of imprisonment for breach of the Law had just been completed, as worthy of admiration and imitation.

It is manifest that such action would be inconsistent with the position of a Magistrate.

In your reply you convey that you only attended as a friend, although on the occasion you presented an address, the wording of which is open to much criticism.

The closing paragraph of your letter cannot be understood, unless, it is intended to discuss the Law, which his Lordship could not for a moment sanction, in considering the propriety of your conduct as a Magistrate.

If the Lord Chancellor thought that your action was deliberately intended to affect the object to which he has drawn attention, he would be quite unable to condone it.

His Lordship however, infers from your letter that, on the occasion referred to, you took part in the proceedings without having present to your mind that your action was inconsistent with your position as a Magistrate, and was calculated to have the effect suggested.

Acting on this assumption he is prepared to allow the incident to close, with however a grave warning to you to be more circumspect in future.

I am Sir, Your obedient Servant,
J Nugent Liutaigne.

The contents of Henry's next letter could not be found by the author, but the reply it received is suitably revealing:

Lord Chancellor's Secretary's Office,
Four Courts,
Dublin

12th Day of August 1902.

Sir,

I am directed by the Lord Chancellor to acknowledge receipt of your letter of 6 August conveying your resignation of the Commission of the Peace for the County of Mayo.

Yours Faithfully,
W M Campbell, Colonel. Private Secretary.

For many years I wondered who the Lord Chancellor was that wrote to my grandfather all those years ago. He was one Edward Gibson (1840-1913), 1st Baron Ashbourne. He came from a Dublin legal family and owned a small estate in Co. Meath. He was Conservative MP for Dublin University (1875-1885), Attorney General for Ireland (1877-1880) and Lord Chancellor of Ireland (1885-1886, 1886-1892 and 1895-1905).

SWINFORD DISTRICT COUNCIL, 1906

The annual statuary meeting of the Swinford District Council was held in June 1906, in the aftermath of Michael Davitt's death. Mark C. Henry, JP, was the Chairman presiding. The following Councillors were also present at the meeting: J. Morrin, M. Igo, J.A. Mellett, T. Morrin, A.J. Staunton, J. Morrisroe, T.F. Harrison, T. Gannon, M.J. McLoughlin, T. Roughneen, J. Parsons, M.F. Campbell, W. McNerney, P.A. Mulligan, P. O'Hara, P. Jones, J. Roughneen and D.J. Murtagh. At the meeting, Mr A.J. Staunton proposed Mark C. Henry for the chairmanship for another year. Mr James Morrin seconded. He also proposed the re-election of Mr Patrick Jones as vice-chairman.

When the business of the meeting was concluded, the Chairman Mark C. Henry said that he now had to perform one of the saddest duties which it had ever fallen to his lot to discharge, namely to propose a resolution of regret at the death of that great Irishman, Michael Davitt, whom they had laid to rest the previous Saturday in the ancient burial ground of Straide. He said he could not recall any occasion which had so deeply moved the hearts of Irish people and sent so intense a wave of sorrow to all classes, as the death of the founder of the Land League, who first pointed out to them the only lines upon which they could work with any prospect of success for the emancipation of the tenant farmers of Ireland. When they remembered the work which he had accomplished and what he could still do, if God had spared him, it was hard to realise that the heart which always beat so warmly for his native land was now stilled in death. Henry stated that Mr Davitt was a unique figure in Irish politics, and he could never be replaced. The only consolation they had was that through his works and writings he would continue to speak to them from beyond the grave, and his memory would be a beacon to move his countrymen to greater effort for the achievement of that measure of liberty which he said it was his life's ambition to obtain.

The Chairman also mentioned that in all the churches in the parish of Charlestown prayers were offered up publicly for the repose of his soul, and he hoped that that noble character who spent his life in the cause of suffering humanity would receive a just reward from that great Divinity that 'shapes all our ends rough hew them as we may'. He begged to propose the following:

Resolved: That we, the Swinford Rural District Council, desire to join in the Nation's profound sorrow at the death of Michael Davitt and to tender to his bereaved wife and children, the expression of our heartfelt sympathy in their affliction.

Resolution: Mr Davitt's death has called forth among all creeds and classes of the community a feeling of grief and sympathy which has scarcely a parallel in the annals of Irish history, while his priceless services to his country, his record as a gifted patriot, and his noble work as a champion of human liberty in all climes, have gathered around his memory a halo of respect and gratitude which will last until the end of time.

We earnestly hope that these tributes of undying affections from the hearts of the people he loved and so unselfishly worked for may help to assuage the bitterness of that great sorrow which has fallen on his afflicted family. I hope it will bring them some small measure of consolation in the hour of their terrible bereavement.

We now adjourn this meeting without transacting any further business, as a small mark of respect to the memory of the illustrious patriot.

Mr James Morrin, Chairman of the Board of Guardians, said it was his mournful duty to second the resolution. Mr A.J. Staunton said he felt it a melancholy duty to support the resolution. Mr Thomas Roughneen, County Council, also said it is his sad duty to associate himself with the expressions of sorrow that had fallen from the Chairman and the other members. Mr J.A. Mellett endorsed all that had been said by the previous speakers.

The clerk of the Union said he would like to have the privilege in joining in the board's expressions of sorrow at the death of this illustrious patriot. He said that the young men of Ireland would always have a guiding light in the life work of Michael Davitt and they would find a fertile source of inspirations in the sacrifices and heroism of his noble career. The resolution was passed unanimously.

The following is a list of some of the people who assembled at different stations along the funeral route and at the graveside in Straide. The body of Michael Davitt was brought from what was then the Broadstone station in Dublin to Foxford by the Midland Great Western railway company:

BALLYHAUNIS STATION
John Hanson, Castlerea.
J.M. Conway.
Conor Flynn.
M.J. Byrne.

The Revd John McDermott, PP, Balla, was among the crowd who stood on the platform at Manulla station as the train sped by. He remained standing with bared head until the train had passed.

CLAREMORRIS STATION
Archdeacon Kilkenny, PP,VG, Claremorris.
Revd Canon McHugh, Crossboyne.
Revd W.J. Browne, CC, St Mary's Greenock.
Revd John Tuffy, CC, Claremorris.
Revd J. McEvilly, CC, Crossboyne.
Revd Patrick O'Connor, Ballinlough.
Revd Father Glynn, CC.
Revd Dr Higgins, President St Jarlath's College, Tuam.
Revd Peter McGirr, PP, Ballindine.
Revd Canon Lyons, PP, Castlebar.
Mr E.P. O'Flanagan, Solicitor.
Mr Patrick McCormack, Castlebar.
Dr McGuire, Claremorris.

Mr Fergus Kilkelly.
Mr Michael Browne, Chairman, Claremorris Board of Guardians.
M.C. Henry, JP, DC, Charlestown.
T.R. McNulty.
P. Moran, Tuam.

CLAREMORRIS AND STRAIDE

M.C. Henry, JP, DC, Charlestown.
T.R. McNulty.
P. Moran, Tuam.
Revd Alex Eaton, St Jarlath's College, Tuam.
Wm Duffy, MP.
John Galvin, County Council.
J.M. Hayden, DC.
M.C. Shine, TC, Tuam.
T. Flatley, Tuam.
M. Nally, DC, Milltown.
T. O'Donnell, County Council, Milltown.

Amongst those present at the funeral at Straide, in addition to those whose names are already given were: Mrs Jordan, Mr John Davitt, Mr Frank Davitt, Mr Hugh Kilty, Miss Margaret Kilty, Miss Mary Kilty (relatives of Davitt, Mrs Jordan being the Godmother of Master Michael Davitt); Mrs Kelly (an old lady, said to be Davitt's Godmother); Very Revd Dr Daly, Ballaghaderreen; Revd T. Walsh, PP Park, Turlough; Revd M. Henry, PP Foxford; Revd M. Gallagher, ADM; Revd M. Keaveney, PP; Revd P. Keaveney, CC; Revd J. Devine, CC Foxford; Revd P. Hewson, professor, Ballina Seminary; Brothers Anthony, Paul, Aloysius, Marist Brothers, Swinford; Revd J.J. McDonnell, PP Killasser; Revd David Humphreys, PP Killenaule, Co. Tipperary; Revd Fr Loftus; Revd J. McEvilly, CC Crossboyne; Revd A. Devine, CC Killasser; Revd Fr O'Connor, PP; Revd J. O'Grady, PP Bohola; Revd P. Hunt, PP Straide; Revd W. Henry, PP; Revd Fr Mullen; Revd Fr Murphy, CC Balla; Revd P.J. Hurst, CPS; P. O'Hara, DC; M.T.J. McEllin; T. Walshe; P.A. Mulligan, Charlestown; J. Morrisroe, Charlestown; J. Davis, JP; R.A. Gillespie, Castlebar; T.H. Gillespie, Castlebar; M. Gallagher, Straide; James Gallagher, Straide; H. McGowan, Duff & Co., Ballaghaderreen; T. Forde, Straide; M. O'Grady, NT Straide, and Francis Davitt, Swinford.

The arrangements in connection with the burial were carried out by

Denis Johnston, who had been in the District for a few days and who was assisted by J. Morrin, County Council, Mr Jones and Mr Boland.

MEMBERS OF PARLIAMENT AND COUNCILLORS

Charlestown had two Members of Parliament in the early years of the Irish Free State – Mark C. Henry TD, of the Square, and Jim Morrisroe TD, of Barrack Street.

The town entered the national political scene for the first time with two general elections in 1927, when Mark Henry went forward as a Cumann na nGaedheal candidate for the constituency of North Mayo and, in being elected to the Dáil in the first election held in June, had the honour of being the town's first TD. On facing the electorate for the second time that year, in the September election Mr Henry was again successful. Henry represented the constituency until 1932.

A new candidate from Charlestown faced the electorate in the constituency of North Mayo in the general election of 1933 in the person of Jim Morrisroe, again a Cumann na nGaedheal nominee. He was then elected to the Dáil, replacing Mark Henry who did not seek re-election. Mr Morrisroe was a brother of the then Bishop of Achonry, and he represented the constituency until 1937.

Both Mark Henry and Jim Morrisroe were members of the Swinford Board of Guardians and the Swinford District Council. Other residents of Charlestown who were on both boards were Messrs J.W. Mulligan, P.A. Mulligan, J. Harrison, J. Parsons, J. Mulligan, and from outside the town, J. McDermott of Bushfield, Frank Davey of Carracastle and T. O'Hunt, Doocastle.

Members of Charlestown electoral area who were elected to Mayo County Council were namely: Mark Henry; John Harrison; William F. Gallagher; Patrick J. Honan; Thomas Tarpey, Clooncoose; Thomas Durkin, the Square; Patsy Dunne, Barrack Street; John M. Flannery, Barrack Street, and Gerry Murray, the Square.

MARK C. HENRY, TD, 1854-1952

Mark Henry was born in Charlestown, Co. Mayo, in the month of July

1854. He was the second son of Michael Henry and Mary Mulligan. His older brother John M. was born in 1852. Mark's father Michael came from Swinford, where his family were involved in the commercial life of that town. Michael's family operated the tolls and customs of the fairs and markets at Circular Road. They also ran a public house and leased other properties from the Brabazon family, who owned Swinford at that time.

Mark's mother Mary was the only daughter of John Mulligan and Elizabeth Haran. John Mulligan was responsible for providing the site and new house in 1846 for the newly married couple. Elizabeth died first and John died in 1876.

Michael and Mary operated what we would today be referred to as a bed and breakfast establishment, for the passing traffic of the early 1850s. But their cosy lifestyle was not to last very long, as Michael died in 1862, leaving the young widow with two sons to raise and a business to run. But Mary did just that and her two sons John and Mark progressed well. John, being the eldest, helped his mother run the business and his brother Mark took himself off to America in the early 1870s to work in a bar on 10th and Chestnut in Philadelphia. He worked for the Griffin family, who were relatives.

Mark married Catherine Carney in America and the young couple returned home to Charlestown at the request of his mother. His brother John was enjoying the good life too much and Mark was badly needed to

Mark C. Henry, TD, Mayo County Council, 1854-1952.

help run the business. Sadly, Catherine died in 1883.

After a time, Mark got involved in local politics and was elected to the Swinford Board of Guardians, the local authority of the period. He was a member of the Charlestown Dispensary District and served on that body until 1894. His brother John died in 1892 and his mother Mary in 1897.

Mark got married for a second time in 1894 to Margaret Filan from Swinford. They had four children: Mary (May), 1895-1984; Michael, 1897-1946; John (Jack), 1898-1990, and James Anthony (Tony), 1900-1982. Margaret Henry died in 1938.

As a small boy Mark had trod the streets of Charlestown, then just a tiny village. He lived to see it grow into a prosperous and forward-looking business town, with every amenity, including its very own Electric Light Company, which was incorporated into the ESB in 1927. Much of the town's early development might be traced to Mark Henry's unflagging energy. No man of his period devoted more time and energy to the service of the people in his native town.

Following the passing of the Local Government Act of 1898, he became prominently identified with public administration, though earlier in 1892, he was elected a member of the Swinford Poor Law Guardians for the Sonnagh division. As far back as 1877, he joined the Fenians, into which he was initiated by the late Jack Carney of Copplecurragh. He attended meetings of that advanced body, forerunners of the organisation which was later to set the seal of freedom on his native land.

While in Philadelphia, he had joined Clann na nGaedheal in 1881, the year that Michael Davitt went to America to seek support for the newly established Land League. He strongly supported Davitt's efforts and later became his intimate friend.

When Mark Henry returned to Charlestown he continued to be an active worker in the movement for a free Ireland. Then Land League yielded to the United Irish League. He was appointed the first Chairman of the local branch and later of the East Mayo Executive. The tenant farmers had in him a staunch and restless friend and champion.

In 1899, one year after the passing of the Local Government Act, he was elected a member of the first Mayo County Council. He remained there for the next twenty years. During this time he was Chairman of the Swinford Rural District Council. He also had to preside at the meetings, including one in June 1906, where, in his own words, 'I have to perform one of the saddest duties, which has ever fallen on me to discharge, namely to propose a resolution of regret at the death of that great Irishman Michael Davitt, who was laid to rest last Saturday in the ancient burial ground of Straide.'

For a considerable time he was also Chairman of the County Board of the AOH, and was one of the pillars of the local GAA club. In his youth he enjoyed the game of handball and often played in the old Bushfield ball alley. He lived to see one of his sons, the late Jack Henry, win national handball titles, win a Sigerson cup medal with UCD in 1923, and play for the Mayo team in the infamous All-Ireland final of 1925.

In 1927, he was elected to Dáil Éireann as a Cumann na nGaedheal member and remained in office for five years, until he retired owing to advancing years. He was 'Father of the House' during this time.

The editor of the *Western People,* writing at the time of Mark's death in 1952, said of him:

> During his long life he made no enemies, but was held in affection and esteem by all, even in the stormiest period of Irish history when so many friendships were strained or broken and when feelings grew so embittered. He passed away leaving pleasant memories of a great Irishman, of unswerving loyalty to the ideals of freedom and to the service of his fellow men. May the sod of the soil he did so much to enfranchise rest lightly on the grave of a true friend, a devoted parent and a sterling Nationalist.

The following are written questions from Henry's time in the Dáil:

20 MARCH 1928, SALE OF CO. MAYO ESTATE

> Mr HENRY asked the Minister for Fisheries if he is aware that the lands held in the name of Thomas Clossick (deceased) by Mary Clossick, of Hagfield, Charlestown, Co. Mayo, is about to be sold by the occupier; and whether he will take steps with a view to the acquisition of these lands by the Land Commission for distribution among the uneconomic holders and landless men of the district.

> Mr RODDY: The lands referred to appear to comprise the holding of 14a. 2r. 31p. situated in the townland of Hagfield, Co. Mayo, which was vested in the tenant the late Thomas Clossick under the Land Purchase Acts and in which there is in consequence an annuity payable. The Land Commission does not

propose to take any action with a view to their acquisition.

2 MAY 1928, NAME OF MAYO TOWN

Mr HENRY asked the Minister for Posts and Telegraphs whether he has received a resolution from the Mayo County Council, passed at their meeting on the 24th March, 1928, requesting the Minister to change the name (now Bellaghy) of Charlestown, to 'Baile Chathail'; whether he agrees to the terms of the resolution; and, if so, when it will take effect.

Mr HEFFERNAN: I received on the 26th April a copy of a resolution passed by the Mayo County Council at their meeting on 24th March requesting that the name of Charlestown be changed on the Post Office official stamps from 'Beal Lathaighe' to 'Baile Chathail'. I have no objection to the proposed alteration and will arrange for the change to be carried out as soon as possible.

7 NOVEMBER 1928, OLD AGE PENSION CLAIMS

Mr HENRY asked the Minister for Local Government and Public Health whether he will state why Pat Grennan, of Orlar, Kilkelly, Co. Mayo, has not been granted an increase in his old age pension, which is presently only 4/- per week, notwithstanding that the valuation of his land is only 5/4.

General MULCAHY: An appeal was received on the 14th April last arising out of a question by the pensioner for an increase of his existing rate of old age pension (4/- a week). It was reported that he lived with his wife, two sons and a daughter on a farm of land (Poor Law valuation, £1 15s 0d) carrying some stock and with some tillage. There is also a shop, the profits from which, including proceeds from egg dealing, were estimated at £40. It was not clear, therefore, on the evidence, that the pensioner's means, as calculated for pension purposes, were less than £31 7s 6d a year, and by a decision dated 11th May, 1928, it was determined that he was not entitled to a pension at a higher rate than 4/- a week.

Mr HENRY asked the Minister for Local Government and Public Health whether he is aware that the Foxford Old Age Pensions Sub-Committee allowed a pension of 9/- a week to John McHale, of Muckinagh, Foxford,

Co. Mayo, which was disallowed by the Pension Officer, and whether he will have further inquiries made, so that the findings of the Sub-Committee will be carried out.

General MULCAHY: This pensioner raised a question about May last for an increase of his pension of 8/- a week. The Balla Pension Sub-Committee allowed a pension of 9/- a week, against which an appeal was received. It was reported that the pensioner owned and resided on a holding of 10 acres (Poor Law valuation, £5) carrying the usual stock. Having regard to all the evidence, it was not clear that the pensioner's means, as calculated under the Old Age Pensions Acts, were less than £20 17s 6d a year, and the application for an increase was disallowed on 16th ultimo. The case cannot now be re-opened.

11 NOVEMBER 1931, MAYO OLD AGE PENSION AWARD

Mr HENRY asked the Minister for Local Government and Public Health if he is aware that the Old Age Pension Sub-Committee at Charlestown, Co. Mayo, awarded an increase of old age pension to Patrick Kelleher, of Doocastle on the 7th October, 1931, against which the pension officer has appealed, and if he will consider granting the increase and confirming the award made unanimously by the Sub-Committee.

General MULCAHY: An appeal in this case has been received. A decision will be given as early as possible.

Copyright Houses of the Oireachtas

SENATOR MARTIN FITZGERALD 1867-1927

Senator Martin Fitzgerald was born in Charlestown in 1867 but moved to Dublin at an early age. He was born in Main Street, in the premises now owned by J.J. Casey known as Casey's Stores, which specialise in hardware. The Fitzgerald family operated a drapery store, and the last registered owner was a Michael Fitzgerald. He or his estate sold the business to the McDonnell family in the early 1900s. Senator Fitzgerald was also known as Senator Martin Tom. He was probably one of the best-known members of the business community in Dublin, as head of the rectifying distillers in Middle Abbey Street. He was also a familiar figure in sporting circles as the owner of several racehorses and a generous patron of sport in general. He was a man of outstanding business capacity and a remarkable character.

During the troubles of Easter week 1916, his Abbey Street premises were destroyed by fire, but with characteristic energy he secured commodious premises in Thomas Street and carried on business while the Abbey Street premises was being rebuilt, a task that took almost four years.

In 1919 Martin Fitzgerald entered the domain of journalism, when he undertook the task of piloting *The Freeman's Journal*. More than once he fell foul of the British authorities. On one occasion he was tried by court martial, ordered to pay a fine of £3,000 and sentenced to two terms of six months imprisonment to run concurrently. He refused to pay the fine and served six weeks of the sentence.

He was nominated by the government of W.T. Cosgrave, as member of the first Senate of An Saorstát. While a member of the Senate, he had heavily involved the issues of import and export duties, damage to property, public accountancy, shop hours (drapery trades) and Oireachtas staff damage. One of his famous statements was, 'If a debt was a debt six weeks ago, it ought to be a debt today.'

He died in March 1927 and left a widow and six children.

MUINTIR NA TIRE, 1953

The following is taken from a report in the *Western People*.

A meeting of the Muintir na Tíre above was held in the Parochial Hall last week [14 March 1953]. Mr Luke Colleran was in the Chair. Among the various matters discussed was a motion by Miss Kitty Mulligan, re repairs to the well on the Well Road. It was agreed that Mr Colleran, Mr Regan and Mr P.J. Brennan would try and find out if it was worth seeing to.

As regards signs for Tample, Knock and Cloonlyon School, the Secretary was asked to write a strong letter to Bord Fáilte and ask that in view of the fact that Knock opens on 3 May, it would be well to have them erected before that date.

Mr Moffitt's proposal re the cemeteries was adjourned, as was the Secretary's proposal that a suitable memorial to the memory of Very Revd

Canon Keaveney be set up.

There was a lengthy discussion on the Mayo rates, proposed by Mr Gannon, Lurga, and the conclusion arrived at was that if we are to have good roads, etc., we must be prepared to pay. The Secretary was asked to write to the County Council, asking them to have the demand notes printed in English as well as Irish.

Very Revd Fr O'Connor informed the meeting that the Land Commission refused to accept the proposal put forward by him for a new weighbridge, and that a new one to be erected would cost £300.

There was a long discussion about the collection of tolls. It was, however, suggested that the tolls should be raised. Mr Weaver said they should be left as they were. Mr Weaver also asked for volunteers to sow alder trees along the Swinford Road. The following agreed to go on Monday at 3p.m., each person taking a spade: L. Colleran, Tony Henry, John Irwin, F. McGuinn, L.

Mayo County Council pictured at the courthouse in 1956. Front row, left to right: Tom Durkin, James Tierney (Staff), Peadar Kilroy, John O'Donnell (County Secretary), Dominick T. Cafferkey, Charles Gilmartin, Liam McLoughlin (County Manager), Sean T. Ruane, T.P. Flanagan (County Engineer). Second row, left to right: Bernard Commons, Joe McManamon, Charlie O'Conner (County Accountant), John Gilligan, Dalgan Lyons, Gertie Devereux (Stenographer), Dr Joyce (County MOH), Paddy Curran, Martin J. Cassidy, Martin McGrath, Jack Garrett, George Egan. Third row, left to right: Unknown, M.J. O'Toole, Bernard Joyce, Michael Kilroy, Joe Sweeney, Tom Bourke, Tony Chambers, Henry Kenny, Tommy O'Hara, Douglas Kelly, Jim Deere (Caretaker), Frank Devaney, Joe Lenihan, Michael Fadden, Peter McGrath.

Weaver and Patsy Dunne.

The Rural Electrification Scheme was then discussed, and Mr Hunt, NT, Carracastle, asked that a deputation from Charlestown and Carracastle should go to Sligo to get the scheme in operation at once. It was decided that once the names were submitted, arrangements should be made for the deputation.

The following were present: Miss K. Mulligan, Mrs T. Henry, Mrs J. Kennedy, L. Weaver, T. O'Connor, J.A. Mulligan, J. Irwin, W. Regan, P.J. Brennan, P. Dunne, V. McGuinn, T. Regan. Mrs Tony Henry acted as Secretary, in the absence of same.

TOM DURKIN, MAYO COUNTY COUNCIL

Tom Durkin was born in Ballincurry, Curry, Co. Sligo in 1903. He was one of twelve children born to Jeremiah and Anne Durkin. Anne's maiden name was Coffey and she hailed from Powelsboro, Co. Sligo. Tom started his working life as a shop boy in McDonnell's Hardware Store, Main Street, Charlestown in 1917, aged fourteen years. His father had to pay Michael McDonnell £50 per year for the privilege. He learned all there was to learn about the business and while there worked with Martin Dunne, who later on opened his own shop in Barrack Street.

His political aspirations then took over, and in 1921 he joined the East Mayo Brigade of the IRA. He stayed with the IRA until 1923 and then returned to work in McDonnell's. Shortly afterwards he left McDonnell's to work for Pat Seary at his hardware store in Tubbercurry, Co Sligo. But Michael McDonnell thought a lot of Tom, and wrote him a letter requesting his return to the Charlestown Store as foreman. Tom duly returned as foreman and performed his duties with Michael McDonnell until 1929. It was then that he took one of the most daring decisions of his life. He rented premises in Main Street, then known as the Railway Bar, from Luke O'Donnell.

The premises had previously been rented by Tom Dooney, a well-known merchant at that time. There was a lot of business in that locality, because of the close proximity of the railway station. There were three trains per day, to and from Sligo. Tom had to start work at 7a.m. to be ready to serve the passengers catching the train to Cobh in Cork, who would then board ships for the long journey to New York, some never to return. Sunday night was also very busy, because of the dances in Walsh's Central Ballroom, just beside him. His brother Charles helped him with the work on many an occasion.

In 1944 Tom was to make another gigantic step in his business life, but before then he experienced many important events. One such event occurred in 1926. In that year, a lovely young girl from Craughwell, Co. Galway, took up a position as bookkeeper in the long-established business of J. W. Mulligan, Bar, Grocery and Hardware Merchants, the Square, Charlestown. She was Bridget Spellman and what an eventful time it was to become for her. Naturally, it did not take Tom long to spot her and, as the saying goes, they started 'doing a line'. That line ended in 1932, when they got married. Their early life was full of happiness, and they were blessed with the birth of six children, four girls and two boys: Maura, now retired in Pine Grove, Charlestown, having given many loyal years to the family business in the Square; Pauline Gorman, now a retired district nurse in Castleblaney, Co. Monaghan; Bernadette Carr, now a retired doctor in Galway; Sheila O'Brien, a retired hotel manageress living in Castletroy, Co. Limerick; Jerry,

This historic photograph of the East Mayo Brigade, Old IRA, was taken outside Swinford church on 7 April 1958, after Mass was celebrated for deceased members. Tom Durkin is fifth from the left in the front row.

a retired businessman who managed the operation in the Square, until it was sold, and last but not least, Joe, now a successful dentist in Ballina.

It was a blessing that Bridget took up her position in J. W. Mulligan's in 1926. Her experience and knowledge of that business probably encouraged Tom to purchase it in 1944. The purchase price was £5000. What a brave decision it was for both of them. To save that kind of money in those days was nothing short of heroic. The premises were purchased from Dr Francis Mulligan, then a doctor in Mullingar.

The two businesses were run concurrently until 1952, when they left the Railway Bar behind and moved to the Square. Many of the customers that they served in Main Street moved with them. The Sligo and Mayo people stayed loyal to Tom during his long career in Charlestown. Some of those who worked for him were: Johnny Doherty, Church Street; Anthony Corley, Corthoon; Mike Cassidy, Hagfield; Liam Brennan, Glann; Seamus Mulligan, Hagfield; Michael Towey, Egool, Kilmovee; Annie and Winnie Kilroy, Church Street; Bridie Mullins and Mary Murphy from near Tuam in Co. Galway, and Bridie Sweeney, Sonnagh, Charlestown. Sadly, some are no longer with us, and are fondly remembered by the Durkin family.

Tom worked hard, but didn't tire, and so his political career commenced. The first Fianna Fáil cumann to be established in Charlestown was in 1926-7 and was set up by Tom, together with P.J. Honan, Jack Peyton, Tiny Duffy, Mike Dillon, Pake Finn and Pake Kelly.

Tom Durkin was nominated by Fianna Fáil in 1955 to contest the local elections in the Swinford electoral area. He shared the Fianna Fáil ticket with M.J. Cassidy and W. Doherty. In the Swinford electoral area there were five seats up for grabs. The electorate was 12,689. The total poll was 8,004; spoiled votes 100, total valid poll 7,895. The quota was 1,316. The candidates and their first count votes were:

M.J. Cassidy, FF outgoing, 1,339.
W. Doherty, FF, 423.
Tom Durkin, FF, 941.
Capt. Thomas Egan, FG, 259.
Thomas Egan, FG, 391.
Eamonn Regan, FG, 427.
F. Turnbull, FG, 215.
P. Walsh, FG, 375.

Douglas Kelly, CnaT, 964.
Tommy O'Hara, CnaT, outgoing, 1,289.
Tommy Tarpey, CnaT outgoing, 656.
Domnick Cafferky, CnaT outgoing. 616.

In his first attempt Tom was elected, along with Dominick Cafferky, Kilkelly, Martin J. Cassidy, Swinford, Douglas Kelly, Swinford, and Tommy O'Hara. Capt. Thomas Egan was from Lavey, Charlestown. Eamonn Regan was from Kilmovee and was married to Olive Gallagher, Charlestown. Tommy Tarpey, was from Clooncoose, near Charlestown, and was an outgoing councillor. Looking back to that election now, it seems that Capt. Egan and Tommy spoiled one another, but that is all history now. Tom Durkin was re-elected again in 1960 and 1967. The Chairman of the County Council in 1967 was Jack Garrett and Tom was elected Vice-chairman. He did not seek re-election in 1974, and handed over the mantle to Patsy Dunne, who won the seat again for Fianna Fáil.

Interestingly, during Durkin's political career there was a rapid decline in the population of the Swinford area. As already stated, the electorate in 1955 was 12,689. By 1967, it had dropped to 9,577, a drop of a staggering 3,112 voters. It must have been very tough for the businesses in the area at that time; thankfully it is a lot better now.

The Durkin family business consisted mostly of heavy and light hardware (including all building materials), timber, iron, cement, furniture, bedding, wallpaper and fertilisers. The bar and grocery also thrived; anything was sold that could be sold, 'from a needle to an anchor'. Deliveries were also very much part of the business and they were made to all of Charlestown and Swinford, as well as Curry, Tubercurry, Aclare, Tourlestrane, Banada and Kilmovee.

Time moved on and Tom passed away in June 1982, his loving wife Bridget dying in 1993. His son Jerry's loving wife Mary (née Carney) died in 2000. Jerry ceased trading in May 1998, and sold the property. He is now happily retired and living in Pine Grove.

Tom Durkin was very much a man of his generation. His quick intelligence gave him a definite grasp of what he could achieve in life and he did just that, from the first day he left Ballincurry, to his last day in the Square of his beloved Charlestown. He understood his role in commerce, family life and politics. He walked into the life he had chosen with dignity, and he left that life never having spoiled his achievements.

As seen in the previous photograph, Tom Durkin attended a 1958 commemorative Mass for deceased members of the East Mayo Brigade, Old IRA. The following members listed also attended:

FIRST BATTALION

Thomas Durkin, centre of picture, fifth from left; P.J. Henry, Swinford; William Foley, Barcull, Kilkelly; Patrick Finn, Carn, Charlestown; Seamus Groarke, Swinford; Sean Robinson, Rooskey, Ballymote; James Gallagher, Brusna, Ballaghadereen; Michael McDermott, Rooskey; Dan Caulfield, Carracastle; Sean Walsh, Cloragh, Rathfarnham, Dublin; Henry McNicholas, Carranteane, Kiltimagh; Patrick Hyland, Trenagleeragh, Kiltimagh; Patrick Dunleavy, No.6 Goldsmith Street, Dublin, and P.J. Honan, Charlestown.

SECOND BATTALION

John Higgins, Sinolane, Ballaghadereen; Michael Mullins, Clooncara, Ballaghadereen; James Carn, Aughaliska, Ballaghadereen; Thomas Price, Killasser; Thomas McNeela, Cloonlumney; Thomas Dunleavy, Meelick, Swinford; John Carroll, Ballinmore; John Charlton, Kiltimagh; Martin Gordon, Sweetwell, Swinford, and Peter Gallagher, Cloonlara, Swinford.

THIRD BATTALION

Thomas Kenny, Kilkelly; Thomas O'Brien, Bushfield, Charlestown; Andy Muldowney, Tullinacurra, Swinford; John Clarke, Bohola; Michael Kilgallon, Culmore, Swinford; Dominick O'Donnell, Ballaghadereen; Michael Lydon, Kilkelly; Michael McGeever, Meelick, Swinford; Joseph Kelly, Ballaghadereen; Patrick Snee, Kilkelly; George Orr, Swinford, and John Mulrennan, Lisacul, Ballaghadereen.

FOURTH BATTALION

Patrick Bolingbroke, Meelick, Swinford; John Finn, Cloontia, Doocastle; Thomas Sweeney, Barnacogue; Peter O'Brien, Ballydrum, Swinford; Jack Regan, Tullinacurra, Swinford; Pat Devine, Midfield, Swinford; Patrick McGowan, Swinford; John Gallagher, Johnsfort, Swinford; John Conroy, Craggagh, Balla, and Frank Colgan, Lucan, Dublin.

SPORT

ALL IRELAND SERIES, 1925

The four-game Dublin–Meath saga in the late 1980s is now part of GAA folklore, and of course, as it captured the imagination of the sporting public, the four games between Carlow and Wexford in 1941 also got considerable airing. It also took four meetings, two of which went to extra time, before the Leinster under-21 final of 1988, between Offaly and Wexford, was decided.

However, what is not generally known outside the west of Ireland is that Roscommon and Sligo had to face each other no fewer than six times in the first round of the Connaught senior football championship in 1925.

The Connaught draw for 1925 paired Roscommon with Sligo and the winners had a semi-final date with the provincial title-holders, Mayo. That left Galway and Leitrim to contest the other semi-final.

The Roscommon–Sligo series opened at Boyle on 17 May. Roscommon won by a point, 2-3 to 2-2, but an objection by Sligo was upheld and a replay was ordered. This took place at Roscommon on 5 July, when the game ended level at 1-5 each. On 19 July Sligo hosted the third meeting and again it ended level; Sligo 0-6, Roscommon 1-3.

These teams returned to Sligo on the 26th of July and once more failed to produce a winner. The next game was held in Roscommon and on August 2nd, Sligo beat Roscommon by 2-5 to 0-5. However, as very often happened in those days, yes, another objection, this time by Roscommon. The objection was upheld, and so on September 13th these two teams met each other for the sixth time, in Roscommon. This time

Sligo won by 2-3 to 0-2 and were through to the Semi-final against Mayo. This game took place in Tuam on October 4th in the old racecourse at Parkmore. Mayo won by two points, 1-6 to 1-4, and qualified to meet Galway in the final.

Because of the delay in completing the Connaught championship, Mayo, the 1924 provincial winners, were nominated to represent the West in the All-Ireland series. They beat Wexford, and Kerry accounted for Cavan in the other semi-final.

Then, believe it or not, Kerry and Cavan were disqualified after an objection, and counter-objection, so that left Mayo the All-Ireland champions, temporarily at least.

The UCD Sigerson Cup winning team of 1923. Back row, left to right: Revd Fr Ryan (Vice-president), G. Hurley, T. Kirby, E. Doherty, P. Mannix, S. Lavan, E.N.M. O'Sullivan, Dr J.M. Ryan. Front row, left to right: P. Downes, E. Carroll, Dr T. Pierse, S. Gardiner (Captain), J. Henry (Vice-Captain), G. Madigan, M. Kilcoyne, T. Ryle, J.D. Grant, F. McNamara, M. McQuaide. Three members of the team – Jack Henry (Charlestown), M. Kilcoyne (Tubbercurry) and 'Baller' Lavan – had Mayo and Connaught links.

Then again came another fateful day in Parkmore, Tuam on October 18th when the Connaught final between Galway and Mayo was held and Galway beat Mayo by 1-5 to 1-3, and, as well as capturing the provincial title, Galway were declared the All-Ireland champions for 1925. What can one say but that another All-Ireland was lost!

The Mayo team of 1925 comprised the following players;

J.E. McEllin (Captain), J. Murray (Goal), B. Durkan, P. O'Beirne, M. Mullins, Fred O'Doherty (Charlestown), J. Regan, M. Mulderrig, J. Forde, G. Delaney, J.J. Walsh, A. Lohan, G. Williams, Jack Henry (Charlestown), and T. Forde.

HANDBALL IN CHARLESTOWN

Charlestown and handball are synonymous. Any discussion of 'the Town' will, sooner or later, evoke the observation that Charlestown always had a reputation of producing handballers, and good ones. This observation is true, and in our boyhood years of the Twenties, a handball and a wall to strike it against was all we needed for our constant pastime.

At that time there was not any regular ball alley, but the big fellows played at Howley's corner, where I now live, the old chapel in Bellaghy, and Henry's hotel corner. We younger fry played at the station, at the various openings off the main streets, and on the back ways.

Handball was also the popular pastime in the area around Charlestown, with three-wall alleys in the villages of Bushfield, Hagfield, Kilgarriff, Egool, Fauleens, Rooskey, Tonroe, Cully, Banada, Cloonfinish, etc. On Sundays these focal points teemed with players, and in the Forties I remember organising a series of tournaments and players from these villages competed.

The obvious question is, 'Why this proliferation of ball alleys in the Charlestown area?' The answer is, to me, equally obvious. The Congested District Board area of East Mayo was notable for the density of its population and its poverty. Some sensitive bristles are now raised by the mention of the word poverty, but I reiterate that there was not only poverty but dire poverty. The people, however, wore their poverty with dignity and in such a setting, an activity that cost nothing except a sponge ball was indulged into the full by the boys and men of the town and country.

The opening of the Handball Alley in 1931. Names of some of those along the back wall are as follows: Luke O'Donnell, J.E. Doherty, Pa Mulligan, Luke Colleran, John Cassidy, Jim Mulrooney, Sergeant Collins, Luke Pa Mulligan, Peter Phillips, Fr Denis Gildea, Mark C. Henry, Bishop Morrisroe, Jim Morrisroe, Bill Gallagher and Willie Joe Burke.

With this plethora of players, the need for a regulation ball court was a crying necessity and in 1927 a Handball Club was formed. The following were the first officers elected: Chairman, Revd Denis Gildea; Secretaries, Tony Henry and Bernie Cassidy, and Treasurer, Willie Moffitt. A committee organised the building of a full standard ball court. Mike Regan of Barrack Street, father of the great Mayo footballer of the Thirties Tommy Regan, was the main contractor. The site was donated from parochial property and the ruins can be seen today behind our new library (the old Town Hall).

The ball court back wall, as distinct from the open three-wall alleys, necessitated the erection of a gallery and amid scenes of great enthusiasm and pride, a great gathering witnessed the official opening of the ball court in 1931, by the Most Revd Dr Morrisroe (a Charlestown man), Bishop of Achonry. Dr Morrisroe also bought and presented to the town the football pitch, known then as 'the Park' in Lavey.

The opening exhibition games were played between the All-Ireland champions Tom Soye and Peter Berry and the O'Rourke brothers of Ballisodare, who played Tommy Marren and Val Harrison. During the Thirties and Forties, Charlestown was full of first-class handballers who competed in some tournaments, but through not having a club affiliated to the County board, were denied county and All-Ireland honours.

In 1947 a new handball club was formed and I was appointed Chairman, with Pa Jo Honan as Vice-Chairman. We held reverse positions in the football club, and the ensuing years were ones of great success and enthusiasm for Charlestown handball and football. To our newly affiliated club All-Ireland honours came quickly. Junior Mulhern and P.J. Doherty won the 1947 All-Ireland minor doubles title, a victory that served as a precedent for a steady flow of county, provincial and All-Ireland titles. In the Twenties the great Charlestown exponent of handballers was Dr Jack Henry, uncle of John and Cathal Henry. He won the UCD and Dublin championships in 1927.

CHARLESTOWN'S ALL-IRELAND CHAMPIONS

MINOR SOFTBALL DOUBLES

1947: Junior Mulhern and PJ Doherty
1949: Kevin Swords and P Bollinbrook
1950: John O'Brien and Tom Hughes
1952: Eddie Tunney and Colm Swords

JUNIOR SOFTBALL DOUBLES

1956: Seamus Fleming and E Connolly
1962: Mickey Walsh and Peter McGee
1980: Martin Hennigan and Partner

NOVICE DOUBLES

1979: M Hennigan and M McDonald

SENIOR SOFTBALL DOUBLES

1966: M Walsh and P McGee

MASTERS DOUBLES
1968: M Walsh and J Walsh
1972: M Walsh and M Groarke
1973: M Walsh and J Gaffney

GOLDEN MASTERS DOUBLES
1978 & 1979: M Walsh and G Daly

NOVICE SINGLES
M. Hennigan

JUNIOR SOFTBALL SINGLES
1971: Brian Colleran

GOLDEN MASTERS SINGLES
1978, 1979 & 1980: Mickey Walsh

SENIOR HARDBALL DOUBLES
B Colleran and P McGee

SENIOR COLLEGES CHAMPION
1963 & '64: Billy FitzMaurice

GAEL LINN SENIOR SINGLES
1968: Mickey Walsh

NATIONAL COMMUNITY GAMES, U13 CHAMPIONSHIPS
1979: Clement Reilly, Seamus Beirne, Martin Kilroy, David Maloney, Stephen Maloney and Martin Gavaghan

Also, Brian Colleran has won many Garda/Army titles and Tailteann games titles.

It is difficult to name every individual in the Charlestown handball scenario, but I will be excused if I name the great perfectionists Mickey Doherty and Mickey Walsh, who, as they synchronised eye, stroke and ball to produce the perfect shot, exemplified the art and skill of handball at its optimum.

As I write, the shadows of Pat Conboy, Danno Regan, Brian Taylor, Harry Frain, Paddy Gavaghan and Kevin Swords, flit across my memory, along with the legions of good, bad and indifferent handballers who graced the ball alley with their efforts and their laughter. There are many omissions to these jottings and I pray to be excused. I was Chairman of the Handball Club for about twenty-five years, and Chairman of the Mayo Handball Board for twenty-one. Over these years the Club and I enjoyed the constant support of Junior Mulhern, Mike O'Donnell, Fr Sean Casey, P.J. Brennan, Mickey Walsh, Ernie Salmon, Patsy Dunne and a host of handballers. My association with handball and the players who played, from juvenile to seniors, remain among my fondest memories.

Jack O'Donnell, 1988

CHARLESTOWN SARSFIELDS

A WRITE-UP OF THE SARSFIELDS AGM OF MARCH 1953

The Annual General Meeting of the Charlestown Sarsfields Football Club was held in the Parochial Hall on Wednesday night. Mr P.J. Honan, Chairman, presided. In his address he extended a hearty welcome to Dr Padraic Carney, who was present. He also welcomed to the meeting Sgt Blythe, who was, he said, an enthusiastic supporter of the GAA and he felt he would be a great help to the club.

Due to circumstances beyond their control, the club's activities were not as numerous as in other years, and due to the small number of teams in senior ranks, the number of games played was negligible. Now that the club had lost eleven of the team that won the junior championship in 1951, Mr Honan felt that it would be only fair to the town and other players, to have them regarded as junior, as it would be impossible, with the material at their disposal to compete in senior ranks.

The Secretary, Mr T. Murphy, reported that the senior team had acquitted themselves very well, being narrowly defeated by Louisburg, beating Ballina, and going under in their only serious defeat to Castlebar, who eventually ran out easy winners over all rivals in the competition. The minor team's activities ended with a defeat at the hands of Aughamore in a knock-out championship. While there was no juvenile championship in East Mayo, the club had a most successful year as regards juvenile football. The club's County Board representative, Revd G. Henry, CC, was instrumental last year in organising teams in every townland in the parish, and on every Sunday and weekday available competitions were held between the different school teams. He was delighted to welcome Dr Carney into the club, and also extended a welcome to Sgt Blythe.

The Treasurer, Mr P.J. Brennan, reported a successful year despite serious losses due to heavy travelling expenses and damages in a court action. Officers elected for the coming year were:

President:Very Revd F. O'Connor, PP
Vice-presidents: Revd G. Henry, CC; Revd P. Higgins, CC; Mr P.J. Honan;
Dr P. Carney, and Sgt P. Blythe
Chairman: Mr Mike O'Donnell
Vice Chairman: Mr Val Harrison
Treasurer: Mr P.J. Brennan
Secretary: Mr Thomas P. Murphy

Visit of Mayo team to Philedelphia in 1963, with Stanley Rowe and Eamonn Walsh, Captain, and the Moffitt and Henry sisters.

Charlestown Sarsfields pictured at a Gaelic park in New York during their trip to the USA (18 September-9 October 1980). Front row, left to right: Brian Moran, Aidan Henry, Tommy Lundy, Pat Walshe, Tommy Colleran, Philip Finn, Pauric Brett, Tommy Halligan, Peter Walshe, Francie Henry. Back row, left to right: Hubert Flannery, Paddy Tunney, Eugene Morrisroe, Declan O'Donnell, Tommy Kearney, Tom Brett, Eamon Brett, John Lundy, John Kearney, Dennis Carney, Fintan Brett, Michael Sheridan, Paddy Murray (inset).

CHARLESTOWN SARSFIELDS USA TRIP, 1980

A large group of Charlestown players, supporters and officials left Shannon Airport on 19 September 1980 at 5.45p.m., on their historic journey to the USA. This was the club's first such trip and everyone was looking forward to visiting New York, Philadelphia, Boston and Chicago. The Mayor of Charlestown at that time was Angela Casey and she said, 'This is a wonderful opportunity to let our emigrants, our children and grandchildren know their town, of which they should be proud.' The officers of the club were:

Patron: Canon E. Gallagher
President: Brian Moran
Chairman: Tom Gavaghan

Secretary: Gerry Hunt
Treasurers: Bobby O'Connell and Marty Horkan
Coach: Paddy Murray
Team Manager: Hubert Flannery
Senior Captain: Tom Kearney
Senior Selectors: Andrew Walsh, Brian Moran, Paddy Murray, Hubert
Flannery and Tom Kearney Fixtures Secretary: Ernie Salmon

The first port of call was New York. Those well to the fore in extending
hospitality were Michael and Martin Griffin who ran the Parkside Tavern
and who were originally from Cloonfinish. Similarly, Padraic, Tom and
Madeline Brehony, who hail from Clooncoose, and who are brothers
and sister of Mrs Kitty Walsh and of Mrs Dolores Horkan, RIP, both of
Charlestown.

Great assistance was also given by: Tommy Murray, brother of the late
Peter Murray, publican; John Murphy, brother of the late Martin Murphy,
garage proprietor; Mrs Vera O'Connor and Mrs Bridget Giuca, who were
formerly Vera and Bridget Tarpey from Clooncoose and sisters of Mrs

John Gallagher, Marty Horkan, Mayor Koch and Paddy Murray, pictured with a
New York City Hall Official on their trip.

Pictured in New York City are, left to right, Marty Horkan, John Gallagher, Veronica Gallagher, John Lundy, Evelyn Healy, Tommy Lundy, City Hall Official, City Hall Official, Paddy Murray, and John Healy.

Maureen Morrisroe; Mrs Nora Nugent, formerly Nora Duffy of Rooskey, whose husband Seamus Nugent was a former Kildare footballer; Eddy O'Hara, who owned several taverns in New York and who is a native of Copplecurragh, and Bill McDonnell from the Bronx, who brought members of the tour party to the Twin Towers of the World Trade Centre, now sadly no longer there.

Others who helped out were: John Fitzgerald, journalist; Pauline and Peter Waldron; Michael Burke; Paddy Duffy; Jim Gilroy; Eddy Webb; Teresa Waldron; Mike Vesey; Eddy Lavan; Mr and Mrs Dominick Frain; Padraic McManus; Mrs Mary Fallon; Paddy Keane; Dinny Molloy; Owen and Mrs McGauran; Attracta Hopkins; Sally Muldoon; Papperins of Woodside, and the Irish Centre proprietors and staff.

SECOND PORT OF CALL: PHILADELPHIA
As in New York, the hospitality in Philadelphia was described as 'fantastic'. There was a function in the Irish Centre, Germantown, after which the touring party broke up to stay with families in the Philadelphia area.

Prominent in the welcoming party were: Mrs Attracta O'Malley, who was formerly Attracta Moffatt from Lowpark; Paddy Gilroy, brother of Eddy, Kevin, and Berny; Mrs Mary Brady; Mrs Bridie Cawley; Mrs Kathleen Ryan; Mrs Maureen Howley; Gerry Lundy; John Mulligan; Brendan Doherty; the Doohan sisters, Mary, Rosaleen, Teresa, and Carmel, and their brother Kevin; Sean Ruane and his wife Mary; Una Devanney; Attracta Vesey; Rosemary Parsons; the O'Grady sisters, formerly from Kilgarriff; Mrs Kate Brennan, sister of Eddy O'Donnell; Mrs Eileen O'Brien; Eddy Cahill; Mike Henry; the Morley girls, formerly from Cortoon; Martin and Sean Feehily; Maureen Gibbons; Joe Cawley, Mr and Mrs Frank Harrington. They were a wonderful group of people and made the stay most enjoyable.

THIRD PORT OF CALL: CHICAGO

The hospitality trail continued unabated in Chicago. The following were to the fore in the welcoming party: Martin Caffrey; J. Dinova; John Hopkins; Peg McGowan; Mike McNicholas; Mike Owens; John O'Reilly, and Frank and Marty Walsh.

FOURTH PORT OF CALL: BOSTON

Boston was also a 'city of the welcomes' and among the welcoming party here were Tom and Sean Stenson, John Cafferty, Bill McGowan, Tommy and Kieran Mahon, and Anthony, John and Brendan Morrisroe. Everywhere the group went, they proved to be great ambassadors for Charlestown. They also chanted our local song, by the late John Healy, who was very proud of his local town:

> Up the Sarsfields, Up the Sarsfields, Up the Sarsfields every time,
> We will meet them, We will beat them,
> Up the Sarsfields every time.

The following is a list of some of the players and supporters who went on the trip: the Kearney brothers, Tom, John and Dennis; the Henry brothers, Aidan and Francie; Brian Moran; Pat Walsh; the Lundy brothers, John and Tom; Paddy and Simeon Tunney; Declan O'Donnell; Miko Sheridan; Philip Finn; Tom Colleran; Tommy Halligan; Eugene Morrisroe; the Brett brothers, Eamonn, Tom, Fintan and Padraic; Peter Walsh; Marty Horkan; Andrew Walsh; Tommy Mulligan; Ernie Salmon; Cathal Henry; Paddy Murray; Hubert Flannery; Bobby O'Connell; Gerry Hunt, and Tommy Finn.

The 1993 Charlestown Reunion Committee. Back row, left to right: Kathleen Henry (*née* Ryan), Nancy and Paddy Kilroy, Attracta Moffitt (*née* O'Malley), Francella Byrne, Rosaleen Doohan (*née* Megonegal), Kathleen Moffitt (*née* Boyle), Johanna Kilroy (*née* McMenamin), Helen Henry (*née* DeGrand). Front row, left to right: Will and Peg Regan, James McIntyre, Mary Vesey (*née* Berman).

ERNIE SALMON

From the early 1940s, the most loyal and dedicated servant of the Charlestown Sarsfields GAA Club has been Ernie Salmon. For any young player wishing to play football in the town, in any era, Ernie has been there, helping them to achieve that end. He has been to the forefront of the club's activities in every decade since, and is a human encyclopaedia of local GAA facts. He has served in every position for the club, depending on demands.

Ernie was born in Charlestown in 1924, the only son of Alf and Catherine Salmon. He was born in the house in Lavey now owned by Pat Caulfield and then by Jane Henry. Alf Salmon was born in Oughterard, Co. Galway in 1879. His father was a teacher, and the family moved to Clifden, from where Alf departed for Charlestown in 1916 to take up the position of postman. As a young man, Alf had joined the British Army and served in India for a few years. Ernie's mother was Catherine McGowan from Montiagh, Curry, Co. Sligo. Catherine and Alf purchased a premises in Barrack Street from Bishop Morrisroe's family in 1926 and started a sweet shop, which stayed in business until 1974. The premises had previously been owned by the Thompson family. When the Eureka Cinema commenced showing the popular films of the day in the late 1930s, Salmon's shop thrived, as did Cassidy's across the street. Many cinema goers in the 1940s and 1950s have very happy memories of buying their favourite sweets in both shops. Alf Salmon died in 1942 and his wife Catherine in 1964. They left a wonderful legacy of happy times, memories of which are still with the older generation to this day.

Growing up in Charlestown in those far off days was very difficult, but life had to go on. Football was one of the outlets that took people's minds off the poverty of the times. It started in the local National School. Games were played around the schoolyard, with teams like Main Street versus Barrack Street, and Fianna Fáil versus Fine Gael.

At St Nathy's College, Ballaghaderreen, which he attended from 1939 to 1942, Ernie made some lasting friendships, such as those with Eamonn O'Hara, Sean Dooney, Mickey Doherty, Cyril Bourke, and Tom Murphy. The President of the College then was Canon Curneen from Aclare and the teachers were Canon Eugene Foran, Fr Tony Foy, Fr Johnny Walsh,

Charlestown Reunion in Philadelphia, 1993.

Fr Jack O'Neill, and Messrs O'Reilly, Collier and Walsh. There were no great football achievements in the College in those days. Ernie left school in 1942 after his father died and went home to help his mother run the shop.

On his return, he got immediately got involved in organising the local minor football team. They often cycled to Tubbercurry for challenge matches. That minor team won the East Mayo final, and went on to the county final, where they were beaten badly by Castlebar by 2-6 to 0-1. This panel of players stuck to their guns and were the foundation of many of the junior teams in the 1940s. The panel of players consisted mostly of the following: Eddie Kilroy, Tom Murphy, Sean Dooney, Pa Joe Webb, Ernie Salmon, Mick Doherty, Gerry and Paddy Walsh, Tommy Fleming, Jim and John Gavighan, Jim and Frank Dillon, John Murphy, Jim Jennings, Cyril Bourke, Pat Barrett, and Tommy Phillips, who was a shop boy in Casey's. In 1947, two juvenile teams were formed, called the Wrens and the Robins, which were the brainchild of Jack O'Donnell. They played many of their games in the old park in Lavey, and this era produced many outstanding juvenile footballers. Players from those teams included: Seamus Fleming, Eugene and Eamonn Walsh, Colm and Aidan Swords, Seamus and Mickey Dunleavy, John Fitzpatrick, Sean Honan, Kevin Honan, Joe Cassidy, Tommy Duffy, Liam O'Shea, Paddy and Michael O'Donnell, Liam Gavaghan, Paddy Cassidy, and Gerry Healy.

The minor team of 1949 was also an excellent team, and the members were: Mickey Vesey, Seamus Beirne, Paddy Henry, Mickey Frain, Tom Peyton, John Healy, Liam Fleming, Bernie Kilroy, Pop Jordan, Kevin Swords, Michael Giblin, John O'Brien, John F. Doherty, Buddie Caffrey, Pake Madden and Tommy Joe Maloney. About this time, Canon Eddy O'Hara came to town, and led the way with Ernie and others to build a new football park in Lowpark. A lot of work went into this project and they created one of the finest and well-laid-out football parks in Ireland. The opening of the O'Hara Memorial Park took place in June 1951. The land was purchased from Bernie Moffitt for £1000. A lot of fundraising was done in Ireland and in America, led by Martin Campbell. Also instrumental in this great achievement were: Eamonn O'Hara, Andrew Walsh, Tommy Phillips, T.E. Henry, Willie Moffitt, Joe Mulligan, Paddy Howley, Val Harrison, Jack Donoghue, Bill Gallagher, Joe Mahon, Jack O'Donnell, John McIntire, and Pa Joe Honan.

From his earliest involvement with the club, Ernie always regarded himself as an administrator. That he was a good administrator is without question, but he also had some excellent people to help him along the way. People like Pa Joe Honan, Val Harrison, Mike and Sonny O'Donnell, Sean Walsh, Brian Moran, Eddy O'Donnell, Tom Blythe, and P.J. Brennan, who was a very efficient treasurer for many years. These men laid a very solid foundation for the club, that was to last well into the future.

Ernie has a special place in his heart for the minor and junior teams of 1953, which both won their respective championships. He regards the junior team of that year as probably the best team Charlestown had had up to then. Prominent on that team were: Dr Padraic Carney; Seamie Fleming; Eamonn, Eugene and Nicko Walsh; Sean Walsh; Eamonn O'Hara; Buddie Caffrey; Colum, Aidan and Kevin Swords; Vinnie Blythe; Sean Honan; Mickey Vesey; Dominick and Seamus Beirne; Willie Regan; Eddy Kilroy; Joe Cassidy, and Jack Foley.

Junior football team of 1951. Back row, left to right: Brian Taylor, Nico Walsh, Colum Swords, Anthony Durcan, Eddie Kilroy, John Caffrey, Willie Regan, Bernie Kilroy. Front row, left to right: Mickie Vesey, Eamonn Walsh, Domnick Beirne, Kevin Swords, Seamus Beirne, Eugene Walsh, Sean Walsh.

Photograph of Charlestown people taken in Birmingham, England in 1962. Left to right: Brian Taylor, Michael Dunleavey, Mrs Son Devanney, Son Devanney and Seamus Dunleavy. The Dunleavy brothers were famous wrestlers in England in the 1960s.

As the years went on, emigration took its toll but the club survived, due to the hard and dedicated efforts of its members. Ernie enjoyed his trip to America in 1980, never resting on the long trip to JFK Airport and visiting New York, Philadelphia, Chicago and Boston.

Charlestown now has a senior team, and one of Ernie's proudest moments was witnessing our county final win in 2001 and gaining the provincial title. Our team reached new heights that year under the astute guidance of Stephen Healy and his selectors.

Today, club affairs are managed efficiently by people such as: Ciaran McBrien, Michael Horkan, Tommy Ward, Tommy Halligan, Ciaran Kilroy, Philly Finn, Margaret Lundy, Kevin James Durkin, and a host of honest workers. The CBD centre is well looked after by Tom Parsons and Rosena Conway. Ernie Salmon is proud of them all and he has left a strong legacy for all to follow. Fittingly his county peers have awarded him with the highest accolades available, namely the Green and Red Trust Fund's Personality of the Year in 1990, and the Hall of Fame Award from the *Western People* in 1995. One of his protégés, John Casey, also won a Hall of Fame Award for Gaelic Football that same year.

Ernie Salmon lived his long life in the present, knowing that in the future, he would most certainly have a place in the past.

ENTERTAINMENT

CHARLESTOWN CARNIVAL, 1949

THE PROGRAMME

Charlestown Carnival

Duration 22 to 29 May 1949

Featuring W.S. Simpson's Amusements & Fun Fair,
including speed-cars, roundabouts, swings, roll 'em in, pongo, shooting range,
la boule side shows, etc.

Gigantic Opening Parade on Sunday 22nd at 3.30p.m.
Ballaghaderreen Boys' Band will attend.

DANCING PROGRAMME

Sunday 22 May – Special engagement of Johnny Cox and his All-Star
Rhythm Band (late of Hangar, Galway) for grand opening dance. Dancing
10p.m. to 3a.m. Admission 5s.

Tuesday 24 May – Bros Walsh, Castlebar, and his Arcadia Ballroom Orchestra.
Dancing 10p.m. to 3a.m. Admission 3s 6d.

Thursday 26 May – Holiday dance with Crystal Dance Band, Boyle. Dancing 10p.m. to 3a.m. Admission 3s 6d.

Sunday 29 May – Grand closing dance. Return engagement of Johnny Cox and his band, Galway. Dancing 10p.m to 3a.m. Admission 5s.

Find Mr X, the Mystery Man, who will attend nightly, and get a free ticket to the closing night dance.

SUPER ATTRACTION ON CLOSING DAY, SUNDAY 29 MAY

The finals of the Mayo Handball Championship at Charlestown Ball Court at 3p.m. Come and see the cream of Mayo's handballers, from Hollymount, Partry, Ballinrobe, Rathduff, Cloongullane and Charlestown compete in the senior, junior and juvenile grades. Minerals and tea stall on grounds.

Visit the different stalls manned by the Ladies' Committee.

Madame Mihalovi Higlovitch, fortune teller awaits your pleasure in Tent 17.

Attractions and novelties, including road and bicycle races will be announced nightly during the carnival.

Proceeds devoted to Charlestown Gaelic Park.

Postcard depicting Charlestown Square in the 1930s.

Carnival procession.

THE ADVERTISERS

P.J. Henry & Co. (Established 1911), Mineral Water Manufacturers, Charlestown.

John McIntyre & Sons, Mineral Water Manufacturers. Proprietor, John McIntyre.

P.J. Honan, Tobacconist, Newsagent and Stationer, Main Street.

Central Restaurant, Main Street. Proprietor, William F. Gallagher.

Howley's, The Square. Proprietor, P. Howley.

James P. O'Hara, Grocery and Spirits, Main Street, Bellaghy.

Jack O'Donnell, MPSI, The Square.

Peter Phillips, Shipping Agent and Undertaker, Main Street.

Olive's Hairdressing Salon, Barrack Street.

McGowan's Cosy Bar, Barrack Street.

James Casey, The Hardware House, Main Street.

Elisha's Hair Salon (including the latest Edwardian Upsweep), Bellaghy.

T.F. Durkan, The Ideal Bar, The Square.

The New Warehouse, Barrack Street. Proprietor, Liam Kennedy.

C.J. Hogan & Son, Retail Merchant, Charlestown.

Parson's Knitting Industry, Barrack Street.

E. Salmon, Refreshments, Confectionery, etc., Barrack Street.

Mark C. Henry, Imperial Hotel & Bus Stop, The Square.

O'Donohue's Bakery, Church Street, Phone 7. 'All that is best in bread.'

Harrison's Select Bar, Barrack Street. 'Value and Satisfaction.'

C.J. Cassidy, Delicious Merville and HB Ices, Barrack Street.

Fitzmaurice Brothers, Butchers, Church Street.

The New Garage, Lowpark. Proprietor, C. Barry.

Fitzmaurice, General Drapers, Bellaghy.

J.F. Mahon, Main Street. 'The house for value.'

Duffy's, Mullard, Phillips, HMV and Pye Radios, Main Street.

Bermingham, Ladies and Gents Tailoring, Church Street.

'The House of Carr', General Drapery and Hosiery, Church Street.

McCarthy's Reliable Bar, The Square.

The Souvenir House, Church Street. Proprietor, Pat Morrisroe.

Michael Doherty, Passport Photographs, Church Street.

Joseph Colleran, 'The Borderline Grocery', Bellaghy.

J.J. Brennan, Tea, Wine and Spirits, The Square.

M.J. Mulligan and his six-piece orchestra. 'They play all the latest.'

Above left: Mary Mulhern and her aunt Mary Gannon, *c.*1950. (*Photo courtesy of Michael Blake.*)

Above right: Pat Blake Sr and his wife, Bridie, baker in Morrisroe's bakery, *c.*1920.

THE ARTICLE

Charlestown, which holds a carnival commencing on Sunday next, 22 May, may be said to be the result of the determination and pride of one man – Charles Strickland. As agent to the Dillon estate, Strickland was a good man and a fair administrator but he was a determined and revengeful enemy if he was once crossed in his dealings. It is said that the Knox family, who owned the adjoining Sligo estate, once slighted him in public, and refused to recognise him as the important personage that he was, and to be avenged, Strickland built Charlestown.

Yet other people say that the people of Bellaghy, living and trading in the Knox Estate, snubbed the traders and farmers from Mayo by making them wait until the end of the market before allowing them to use the scales to weigh their produce, thus crippling them in their trading. Whichever reason is the more feasible, both acted as an incentive to the building of Charlestown.

One day Strickland announced that he wanted six houses built, adding that the man to complete the first house, would receive sixty acres of land at a shilling an acre, along with having the house rent free forever. Carpenters and slaters worked feverishly, and in a short period the race developed into a two-house struggle. Tradition has it that one set of carpenters and slaters got drunk in the final effort, and their nearest rivals – those building Henry's – finished first, the owner thus qualifying for the prize. The year was 1846.

Strickland, determined to have his revenge in full, decided to hold a market, and as the farmers from Bracklough, Tample and Curry trudged down with their produce, picking their way nimbly through the marshy ground on their way to Bellaghy, they found a scale erected near the first house – Henry's. This was three years after Strickland decided to have his revenge. This damaged Bellaghy, and Knox was worried, so worried that he instituted proceedings against Strickland and did his utmost to prevent him from securing a patent for his scales. He was successful, but Strickland, shrewd man that he was, evolved his 'driving a coach and four' through Parliament. He took down the scales from one place as the court ruled, but erected them in another place, quite lawfully. Knox found the instituting of actions for every new scale too costly and he admitted defeat. Strickland's revenge was complete.

He then got to work with a vengeance to erect a town out of the bog. The parish chapel was in Bracklough. Strickland wanted it in Charlestown, and so he put contractors to work. So eager was he to have Mass said in it, that he did not wait to have the church completed. Fr Higgins, the then parish priest celebrated Mass before the floor was completed, and the contractors left without finishing it. Soon afterwards however, a perfect floor was installed. The town was growing fast for three years afterwards and by the year 1849, forty houses had sprung up.

The name Charlestown was given it, as the landlord was Charles Dillon. Later on it was called Dillonstown, but as the people came to admire and respect Charles Strickland, the more they reverted to the former name of Charlestown, because they felt it their duty to commemorate the name of the man who had founded the town.

Strickland was methodical in everything he did, and as the public houses were being built he ensured that they were arranged so that the publican had a separate entrance, other than the one through the Bar. This was done with a view to trading after hours and so that the publican could entertain visitors. In the event of prosecution the case was dismissed, as Charles Strickland was also Justice of the Peace and in that role was very accommodating.

As a result, today's Charlestown boasts thirty-eight bars, an enormous number compared with the size of the town. The Charlestown of today is a model town, for as readers will see from the advertisements to follow, it boasts of a very big business life. Foremost in this respect are its industries. The oldest industry in the town is Donohue's Bakery, established over sixty years ago by James Donohue, father of the present owner, Mr Jack Donohue. The industry has a large clientele all over Mayo.

In a town of so many public houses, two mineral water factories have been erected, one by Mr P.J. Henry and the other by Mr J.J. McIntyre. The year 1911 saw the erection of Charlestown's second oldest industry, P.J. Henry's mineral water factory. Since then their name and their products, including wines, have reached the furthest end of Connaught and today the industry still flourishes, despite post-war conditions. The more recently erected factory is McIntyre's of Lowpark and its products, mineral waters and stout, enjoy a large clientele also, and the industry is expanding to meet demand. Both factories have recently installed the latest and most up-to-date machinery and are providing considerable employment in the district. Also giving employment is the twenty-five-year-old knitting industry owned by Mrs M. Parsons. Although badly hit during the war years, it is now able to meet the demands of the public more easily.

The town is well laid out, with excellent circular roads and a square, reputed to be the largest in Ireland. Its wide streets know no traffic problems.

Charlestown, with all its great facilities, is still forging ahead to even greater heights, and its latest enterprise is truly a noble one and one which is backed by the majority of the town – the building of a new GAA Park. Led by its newly appointed parish priest, that well-known Gael Very Revd Fr Edward O'Hara, the town purchased nine acres of level land in Lowpark and undertook the gigantic task of erecting a park second to none in Connaught. The park is in its final stages and will be completed this week. It is a sign which pays just tribute to the energies expended by the people of the town and particularly by its great and enthusiastic leader, its kind and homely parish priest, Very Revd Fr O'Hara.

Funds are needed to clear the enormous debt and this problem is being tackled in typical Charlestown style by the organisation of a Monster Carnival. The spirit of Charlestown's business people, who have advertised in this page, shows their wholeheartedness to make the carnival a success. They have shown that they appreciated the work of the pastor and that they support the aims and ideals of the GAA organisation, which is going ahead to make the Carnival a memorable one, with parades, novelties, fun fair and an excellent dancing programme.

And as Charlestown starts its second century of business life, it is keeping abreast with the march of time. Its founder Charles Strickland must be smiling as he sees the spirit of determination and pride, which were so characteristic of himself, being maintained and carried ahead by this generation of Charlestown people. And as Charlestown embarks on its second century may we say, 'Charlestown good luck and may God bless all in it and what they do – now and forever.'

'Kipper'

'KIPPER'

In May 1949, the committee in charge of organising the carnival asked the new reporter from the town to write an article in support of the forthcoming event. That young reporter was the late John Healy, one of Charlestown's most famous sons, who had joined *The Western People* the year before. In those days John wrote under the pseudonym 'Kipper'.

After writing this short history of the early years of the town, John then moved to Dublin in 1950. He joined the staff of the Irish News Agency and later on joined *The Irish Press*, before joining *The Irish Times* in 1959 to become the youngest national editor, running the *Sunday Review*, and going on to edit Ireland's oldest paper, *The Evening Mail*. He continued his association with *The Irish Times* as a contract journalist, with one short break, until the summer of 1988 when he agreed to write for the Independent group of newspapers.

Once described as 'the father of modern Irish political journalism', Healy was elected Mayoman of the Year in 1967 and was also voted TV scriptwriter of the year in 1967. He was a Trustee/Director of the Matthew Gallagher Royal Hibernian Academy and the Paul O'Dwyer Forestry Trust. The National Theatre commissioned a stage presentation of his book *Death of an Irish Town* and it was scheduled for the Abbey's 1989 spring programme.

FOR THE RECORD

The following are the list of names of the park committee which helped to make the Fr O'Hara memorial park what it is today: E. O'Hara, A. Walsh, T. Phillips, T.E. Henry, W. Moffit, J.A. Mulligan, P. Howley, P.J. Honan, V. Harrison, J. Donoghue, W. Gallagher, Canon O'Connor, J. Mahon, J. O'Donnell, and J. McIntyre.

Convent girls on a visit to Enniscrone in 1959: Margaret O'Connor, Kathleen Blake, Attracta Moffitt, Finola Bermingham and Patricia Mulligan.

McNulty family of Dennis Day. Left to right: John Owen, Patrick (Dennis Day), Marie with James on her knee, Mary Grady (mother of Dennis Day), Patrick Joseph McNulty (father) and on his knee, Francis Anthony McNulty, father of Barbara Buzynski, who was kind enough to produce these wonderful photographs.

DENNIS DAY, MOVIE STAR AND SINGER

Dennis Day was a popular star of radio, screen and television in 1950s America. He was born Owen McNulty in the Bronx, New York, on 21 May 1918. His father was from Co. Armagh and his mother, Mary Grady (sister of the late Annie Parsons of Palm Cottage, Charlestown), was from Barroe, Carracastle, Charlestown. Dennis Day's first cousin Mrs Mary Phillips lives in Main Street, Charlestown, with her family.

Dennis was married to Peggy Almquist at the lovely Mission San Juan Capistrano in Southern California in 1948. They had three children, Patrick James, Dennis Jr and Michael. Dennis Day's brother, James V. McNulty, Hollywood gynaecologist, was married to the famous American movie actress Ann Blyth in 1953. Some of the famous people at their wedding were Bing Crosby, Joan Crawford, Joel McCrea, Lou Costello and Bob Hope. They were married by his Eminence Cardinal McIntyre, Archbishop of Los Angeles, and a

Dennis Day.

message of greeting from his Holiness the Pope was read.

Dennis Day was happiest when singing. As a boy he sang in the choir of St Patrick's Cathedral, and later when studying for a career as a lawyer he sang for pleasure, but when attending Manhattan College for his degree, he fell seriously ill, and was forced to abandon school and studies for a year. It was during this time that he turned to singing seriously. When he regained his health, he auditioned for radio station WHN in New York and was accepted as a regular on one of the station's programmes.

A short time later he learned that Jack Benny was searching for a young tenor to replace Kenny Baker on his show. Dennis made a record, which he sent through devious channels to Jack Benny, who signed him on a long-term contract. Dennis appeared in many film musicals, such as *Girl Next Door* (1953), *I'll Get By* (1950), *Music in Manhattan* (1944) and *Golden Girl* (1951). He had his own television show in 1952, and he appeared many times on the Jack Benny Show in the 1960s. He also made notable guest appearances on such programmes as 'The Lucille Ball Show', 'Burke's Law', and 'Alfred Hitchock Presents', among many others. Day was also a guest star on the London Palladium Show in 1952, shortly before his famous concert in the parochial hall, Charlestown, on 1 August 1952. The *Western People* advertisement for the concert read:

Meet in person
DENNIS DAY
Hollywood's singing star,
In a Celebrity Concert,

In the Parochial Hall, Charlestown,

On Friday, 1 August, 1952.

Well-known Dublin, provincial and local artists also contribute in a Star Studded Programme.

Doors Open: 8.30p.m. Programme commences 9p.m.

Admission, 5s. Reserved, 3s and 2s.

Join us in welcoming home to Charlestown America's favourite radio singer.

The hall was packed to the doors, a tribute at once to the committee in charge, and to the chief guest artist of the evening, Dennis Day. Dennis was of course the big magnet of the evening and what a generous contributor he was. He spoke, he told yarns, and he danced an Irish step dance with rare artistry.

He sang song after song, one of them was 'Never' from a film in which he appeared. Then he rendered 'My Wild Irish Rose', 'The garden where the praties grow', 'Panis Angelicus', 'Ave Maria' and many others. He was in the possession of a lovely tenor voice, heard to best advantage in 'Panis Angelicus' and 'Ave Maria'.

Next most impressive contributions to a splendid evening were the songs of Winifred O'Dea, the well-known Dublin soprano, and repeated feiseanna cup winner. She gave the audience a wide range of songs, such as 'Scenes that are Brightest', 'My Hero', 'Love and Music' and 'Invitation to the Dance'.

The opening item that night was an orchestral selection by Mick Mulligan's orchestra, which was tuneful and pleasing. A group of young girl dancers from the Duffy School of Dancing, Charlestown, showed well-trained talent at its best.

Mr Frank Connerton, another local contributor, sang 'Love thee Dearest' and 'The Harp that Once' very sweetly and enhanced his reputation as a popular voice. Mr P. Coyle, Kiltimagh, was in excellent voice in his singing of 'Legion of the Lost', 'Bless this House', 'The Ould Side Car', and 'End of a Perfect Day'.

Instrumental duets, piano-accordion and violin, were by Messrs Edward O'Keefe and Martin McIntyre. They were highly enjoyable, skilful contributions to the evening. Fr Joe Higgins, Ballaghaderreen, sang 'My Dark Rosaleen' by special request and was, as always, the finished musician and vocalist.

THE CONCERT

New ground was broken at this concert by a very pleasing interlude, when excerpts from *Hamlet* were presented, with Bernadette Henry of St Louis Convent, Kiltimagh, as Gertrude, Queen of Denmark, and Messrs Joseph Cassidy and Desmond Henry, who learned drama at St Nathy's College, Ballaghaderreen.

It was an impressive, colourful and faultless production. Miss Maureen Dillon was the very accomplished piano accompanist throughout the evening, her piano recital as part of the programme, revealing her real skill and technique as a pianist of a very high order. Mr J. O'Donnell, MPSI, was an ideal Master of Ceremonies.

Just before the national anthem, Fr P.A. Higgins, CC, Charlestown, in the absence of the parish priest Fr O'Connor (who was on a pilgrimage to Lourdes) expressed gratitude to the artists for their services and to the big audience for their patronage.

Dennis Day will always have a warm place in the hearts of Irish men and women and they should never forget his wonderful tenor voice. He loved his native place, a gift given to him by his lovely mother Mary, a proud woman from Barroe. His day in Charlestown, so long ago, will never be forgotten. Dennis Day died on 22 June 1988, in Bel Air, Calfornia.

THE EUREKA CINEMA

Growing up in a small town in the west of Ireland during the Second World War was generally a rather uneventful experience. With virtually no transport, and only Radio Éireann and the three national papers (which were highly censored) to keep us in touch with the outside world (i.e. beyond our nearest town), it was easy to see why our local cinema, or picture house as we knew it in those days, became the focal point of our young lives.

The Eureka, which had opened its doors at the start of hostilities in late 1939, was originally a private house in our street, directly across from our own home. It was owned by four members of a long-established business family in the town, that of P.A. Mulligan. All of them were in their late fifties and early sixties, and each of them contributed to the actual day-to-day running of the concern.

Louise and Marian, having retired from the family trade, were front of house – the former collected the admission fee and issued the tickets from the twelve-inch square window of a small room just inside the front door and later functioned as usherette in the balcony, where the 1s 4d top-class, leather tip-up quality seats were situated.

Joe, the oldest brother, was at the downstairs entrance, to the rear of which were the 9d timber forms, with backs, and the 4d children's backless forms to the front. He doubled as chief ticket-tearer, checker-in and issuer of passes out during performance. His brother Luke mingled throughout the venue, greeting patrons, with a special welcome for his friends whom he escorted to their seats. He dealt with crowd control before the film and, armed with his massive torch, attempted to quell the shouts and ribald remarks of some of the rowdies amongst the 9d seaters during the screening, by spotlighting the danger zones (usually to little or no avail). In fact there were occasions when the melee was so bad that the film had to be stopped and the main hall lights put on before order could be restored. Luke also worked as an undertaker and prepared his coffins in an upper room adjoining the balcony entrance. Many a newcomer to the 1s 4d seats, on opening the wrong door, could find themselves confronted by an open casket on low trestle supports, surrounded by all the trappings of burial.

Another brother, the gregarious cigar-smoking Paddy, was a solicitor in Ballina. He owned two Estoria cinemas, one in Ballina and the other in Galway. As he did the booking for both places, he also included the Eureka, and consequently we got the first films straight from Dublin, before all the smaller towns in the area. This resulted in large queues from time to time. I can recall a long line of people trying to get in to see *The Song of Bernadette* and *Going My Way*.

The weekly programme was advertised on a small poster and in the local newspaper, the *Western People*, but most patrons relied on the town's bellman, John Irwin, to bring them the glad tidings of the night. About an hour before opening time, at around 7.30p.m., John toured the streets ringing his huge bell, and in his great stentorian voice announced through his homemade tin megaphone to one and all the latest picture show, always straight from Hollywood. He started every announcement with an earth-shaking, 'Hear ye, Hear ye, Hear ye', and ended on the same attention-grabbing note with 'Don't miss!'

Every household in the street knew when it was 'Doors open', as the lovely voice of John McCormack singing 'Where the Shannon River Meets the Sea' came scratchily across the outside speakers. I often wondered why they always started with this particular song, but never had the courage to ask. The same six tunes were played in the same sequence for many years before the 'nine o'clock sharp' transmission.

Because the operator in the projection room worked his day job in my father's business, I easily fell in as his enthusiastic dogsbody. My main task was to collect lead-covered boxes of film reels which arrived on the daily train from Dublin. I had to be on the ball and deliver them promptly, as in those days, for some reason, all the reels had to be rewound before showing. Two projectors were used, and during the changeover from one reel to another, Murphy's Law sometimes took over, with reel No.3 coming before No.2. As you may imagine this proved to be a bit confusing for the patrons, and they were known to vent their disapproval by letting off stink bombs.

Many times the train was very late, and the patrons had to wait up to an hour before proceedings could start. No one seemed to mind – least of all the courting couples in the back rows. I also had the task of putting up the 'stills' on the walls of the foyer. These were action photos of the stars in scenes from their current films. At Christmas time, when a full two weeks of non-stop favourites were being promoted, I had to hand out a small two-page cardboard programme of events. Near the end of the last page you would inevitably receive the following advice 'If you see *We Recommend*, this means something special is in store for you, but if you spot *We Definitely Recommend*, be prepared to have your mind blown away!'

The heating in the cinema consisted of a small circular paraffin-heated stove placed in the front of the balcony, hence the clamour for rows A, B and C. The right aisle seat, beside the heater, was kept for the local dance-hall proprietor, a friend of Luke's, and the four seats behind him in row B, for the manager of the local bank and his family, all avid cinema goers. Those patrons seated behind these rows, viewed the 'spectacles of the century' through icicled lashes, unless they came prepared with overcoat, scarf, gloves and fleece-lined boots. Downstairs warmth was provided by a large cast-iron turf-fired heater along one wall, towards which early picture goers gravitated. This area also included the heaviest smokers and critics, who had a very effective way of expressing their disapproval of some scenes; by collectively banging the timber floor. The wave of cigarette smoke arising from this region made for rather blurred viewing for those at the back.

Air conditioning was unheard of in those days. Open windows on one side was the only ventiliationt and this only during a heatwave. However, the breath of air may not have lasted too long, as the noise of the *Battle of Atlanta* awakened the neighbour's child and the shutters had to be closed again.

My brother and sister and I, in our early years, were taken to the balcony by our mother, clustered together in the middle rows, clad for the Klondike, under a Foxford rug and boosted by a hot water bottle which we all shared. Comfortably ensconced in those torrid conditions, we could indulge our fantasies with our heroes and heroines on the screen: Hopalong Cassidy, Gene Autry and Roy Rogers riding to the aid of damsels in distress; James Cagney and Humphrey Bogart shooting it out in the gangster scenes, with the Dead End Kids tagging along. *The Roaring Twenties* and *Angels with Dirty Faces* were our favourites and we enjoyed the funny antics of the Marx Brothers, Laurel and Hardy, and Abbot and Costello, not to mention and the death-defying deeds of Errol Flynn, the number one star of the day … enchantment!

During the war, in order to help live theatre artists, the Government introduced Cine-Variety. This meant that each film showing had to be preceded by half an hour of live theatre consisting of local musicians, singers, dancers, reciters, etc. This was often more popular than the films that followed, but the performers regularly had to contend with the hisses and rude remarks of some impatient cinema goers, eager to see their screen heroes.

Before the main feature film we always had 'shorts'. These would last between five and fifteen minutes and we would usually have three. These were followed by the Pathé newsreel, giving us the world's war news of the week. We did not realise it at the time but of course it was propaganda, and it must have influenced our thinking in future life. The news might be followed by a nature programme and lastly came the trailer for the forthcoming 'blockbuster from America'. From time to time we were treated to a 'double feature'. This would consist of a 'B' movie, which would be somewhat shorter than the principal one and generally had second-rate actors.

My Mum's favourites were the musicals – particularly those with Judy Garland and Deanna Durbin – and the 'weepies'. Our household was saddened for days at the death of Bette Davis's character in *Dark Victory*. But most of all it was the humorous capers of the comedians that stayed with us as we attempted, in our tin-pot way, to imitate them during our leisure hours.

As the emotionally drained and laughter-laden patrons departed nightly from their darkening picture house, leaving their dream worlds behind, they would fortify themselves in Mrs Salmon's nearby sweetshop with brown paper bags of bullseyes, a packet of five Woodbines (if they were lucky) and one of Mrs Salmon's delicious homemade vanilla ice creams. They would then retrieve their bicycles, which they had parked against the walls of many of the local houses in the street, much to the chagrin of the owners, and prepare themselves for the real world. Strangely enough during all those years I never once heard of a bicycle being stolen or even damaged. Mounting their Raleighs they would ride, John Wayne style, into the sunset, complete with holstered cycle pump on the rear upright bar and claw-like spurs clasped around their trouser bottoms for protection.

The charming, old-world, owner-managers of the cinema have long passed on but the friendly welcome and happy smiles with which they greeted each patron will be remembered for many a long day. The highly rouged face of Louise in the box, always good for a free pass for the 'skint' regular; Marian, heavily coated and booted, chain-smoking away as she managed to squash you into a packed balcony seat; the lightly built figure of Joe, precariously perched on his high timber stool, ever eager to discuss the news of the day as he split the Parterre tickets, and Luke, forever the genial host, filling you in on the night's presentation, before slipping out to T.B.'s adjoining hostelry for his nightly scotch and soda. To those family members who dedicated their twilight years to bring us so much enjoyment, we owe an immense debt of gratitude.

Sadly the Eureka, our childhood lifeline to the world, is no longer in use. Like so many cinemas in rural Ireland, it closed its doors in the early sixties, a casualty of television. It has since housed a knitting business, a tool-manufacturing workshop, a second-hand furniture store and I have recently seen a notice on the front door seeking planning permission for apartments.

Who knows what the future holds for the site. But for those of us who grew up during the Emergency and the immediate post-war years, it still represents the happy-go-lucky days of our youth, for there we discovered another magical world, which, even if only for a few fleeting hours, sustained, enlightened, and captivated us during those halcyon times over half a century ago.

Paddy Henry

The late Paddy Henry.

PERFORMERS

One Charlestown entertainer, never to be forgotten, was the late Michael 'Mick' Mulligan of Hagfield. Mick was born on 12 December 1924, one of three children born to Michael and Margaret (*née* Corley). The other two children were Mary and John.

Since there was no TV to watch in those far-off days, radio was the only means to hear what was going on in the outside world. In his teenage years Mick would listen to the radio frequently, especially music from around the world and America in particular.

He was very interested in the masters of swing from America, and the likes of Artie Shaw, Benny Goodman, Tommy Dorsey and Glenn Miller influenced him greatly. Some of the Jazz legends like Buddy Rich, Mel Tormey, Gordon Jenkins and Billie Holiday were also on his agenda. Mick was a self-taught saxophone player and completed his musical training with the trombone. He was also a music teacher and band director, and many young men around the Charlestown area were taught by him, and greatly influenced by his direction.

By the late 1940s Mick had his own six-piece orchestra, and one of his first engagements would have been in the old Town Hall, now our local library, in May 1949. A carnival was organised in the town to help raise funds for the new Gaelic park and he would have shared billing with the likes of Brose Walsh, The Crystal Dance Band (Boyle), Tony Chambers (Newport), and Johnny Cox and his band from Galway. The late Michael Carr of Church Street was Mick's transport man and would have driven him and his band all over the country.

Mick's passion was music, and his orchestra quickened the pulse of a generation, from the late 1940s to the late 1950s. His music helped people to shrug off the poverty and depression of those hard times. Other popular orchestras at the time would have included those of Mick Delahunty and Maurice Mulcahy.

In the 1950s, most of Ireland's entertainment was provided by these 'orchestras', which were really just dance bands with between ten and twelve musicians. They played a mix of standard tunes and pop; their music was danceable, and if you could not dance then you would not get the lady!

Then in came the Sixties and everything changed. Younger people wanted something different and exciting and they got it. The Showband era arrived and once again, as happened in the 1940s, American influences played a part.

'Christmas greetings from the Fab Five', this time with Vinnie Egan on bass guitar and vocals.

The Showbands brought modern pop music to our shores, and all the new songs were sung in halls all over the country. Who were the first? Well, the Clipper Carlton are credited with starting the rage, although the Dave Glover Band were close behind. Their music was a mixture of rock and roll, pop and country and singers like Frankie Avalon, Fabian, Johnny Ray, Buddy Holly, and Bobby Darin (not to mention English singers like Cliff Richards, Billy Furey and Adam Faith) influenced our artists greatly.

Mick Mulligan needed to adapt quickly to the new sounds and that he did. As I mentioned earlier, he was a teacher and master of music. He encouraged many young men in and about Charlestown, and if they wanted to learn, he taught and organised the bands. In the early sixties he formed bands like the Dixietones, the Fab Five and the Fiesta Showband.

The Fiesta Showband was formed in 1969 and its members were: Mick, band leader and saxophone; P.J. Foley, vocals and guitar; Michael Murphy, drums and trumpet; Vincent Doherty, bass guitar and vocals; Pat Blake, rhythm guitar and vocals, and last but not least, Brendan Walsh on guitar, accordion and vocals. They dressed in red jackets, white polo shirts and white pants. They once played in the Central Ballroom, Charlestown, in front of over 700 people. They also shared top billing with Big Tom in Swinford Town Hall on one famous night.

The Dixietones Showband. Left to right: John Foley, Mick Mulligan, Patsy O'Grady, Sean Tiernan, Shay Cribben and Mal Tiernan.

The members of the Pasadena Showband, Ballina: Johnny Popp, leader, trombone and vocals; Michael Healy, tenor sax, clarinet and vocals; Tommy Kelly, lead guitar, harmonica and vocals; Dermot Hopkins, lead vocalist; Paddy Moran, drums and vocals, and Jerry Duffy, bass guitar and vocals.

Later on in the early seventies, the Fiesta was renamed the Western Dixie Flyers and was managed by Eamonn Walsh. P.J. Foley became the 'Tall Texan', and was in great demand all over the west. During the late Sixties, it was common for artists to change bands and one resulting band, which achieved fame all over Ireland, was the Riviera Showband. In 1967 its members were Patsy Haugh, Gerry Foley, John Conway, Brendan O'Grady, Kevin Maloney and Shay Cribben. This band was managed by Seamus Cox. Kevin Maloney had a hit with Johnny McCauley's 'The Latchyco', Shay Cribben with 'Love and the Country' and Malachy Tiernan received several plays on Radio Éireann. Malachy, Gerry and Brendan would later on form the group Roots and played the singing lounges and dinner dances in the area.

Andrew Walsh Senior pictured in 1950.

The Walsh Family Band: Nicko, sax; Betty; Andrew, sax; Eamonn, drums; Mickey, trumpet; Carmel, singer, and Eugene, violin. Frank is missing from photo.

As previously mentioned, Andrew Walsh Sr established the Central Ballroom in the 1940s. He had to compete with the Town Hall and all the other venues in the area, and that he did, with great gusto. If a band ever failed to turn up, Andrew had the answer – his own family. The family band comprised: Nicko on sax; Andrew Jnr on sax; Eamonn on drums; Mickey (a cousin) on trumpet; Carmel on vocals, and Eugene on violin.

During this very musical era in Charlestown, a group was formed in the town called The Four Shamrocks, the members of which were Frank Connerton, John Mahon, Sean Honan and Seamie Fleming. Their hits included 'Cool Water', 'Goldmine in the Sky', 'A Mother's Lullaby', 'Hannigan's Hooly' and 'Galway Bay'. They were very much in demand on the radio at that time. Frank Connerton sang with many bands as the demand presented itself, once singing with Maurice Mulcahy in the Town Hall. The ladies also had their singers, like Ita Carr and Maureen McGowan.

The Walsh family. Back row, left to right: Angela, Nicko, Betty, Mickey (nephew), Louise (mother), Andrew Jnr, Eamonn, Eugene, Carmel, Andrew Snr. Front row: Dolores, Emmanuel.

The Four Shamrocks. Left to right: John Mahon, Seamie Fleming, Sean Honan and Frank Connerton. The photograph was taken in Mahon's house in 1956.

Left: The Fab Five, featuring Mick Mulligan (tenor sax and bass guitar), Brendan Walshe (drums), Kevin McDonnell (lead guitar and vocals), Gerry Walshe (rhythm guitar and vocals), and Patsy Foley (bass guitar and vocals).

Below: Mike Doherty and family of Church Street. Left to right: Johnny, Mickey, Tommy, Fr Padraic, Maureen, P.J., Mike.

In earlier times, one of the first masters of music was Pat Brennan of Church Street. He was father of Annie, Tom and Pete. He had a pipe band in the town, with Tom, Pete and Mike Doherty (father of Vincent), on big bass drum. John Irwin was also a well-known traditional player, and his son Peter was the Town Crier. Mr Giblin was a music teacher in those days and Delia Gannon, mother of Seamie Fleming, was also a beautiful singer. Frank Connerton remembers with fondness Pete Browne and his band of renown and Dick Prendergast, Kilkelly.

Mick Mulligan, who went to his eternal reward in July 2002. He had great singers, great songs, great arrangements, and above all, he was a great leader. He left a wonderful legacy to his fans, to his friends and to his beloved wife Evelyn and children, Fiona and Michael.

MEMORIES OF CHARLESTOWN

MY NEIGHBOURS IN CHURCH STREET

I was born in Charlestown on 16 May 1941, the eldest son of Tony and Delia Henry. I was actually born in the house now occupied by Miss Bernie White. In 1941 the house was owned by a Martin Foy from Swinford. It was later sold to Willie Moffit and he in turn rented it to Joe White, who was a shoemaker by profession. My father helped his sister May run the family business, which was then known as the Imperial Hotel. It consisted of a bar, grocery, accommodation and a hackney service. My mother, who was Delia Lenihan from Killaturley, was a National School teacher. She taught in Cloonlyon, Tavneena and Barnacogue National Schools.

Our next-door neighbour was Bea Cryan, whose lovely song, which she sang regularly, was called 'Memories'. Next to her the Morrisroe family moved in sometime in the mid-1940s. Pat and Molly ran a toy and grocery shop. Across the road from the Morrisroes' house lived Jim 'Laddy' Mulrooney and his family. Then the O'Hara family moved in. Evelyn and Eamonn ran a shop, which later on became the famous Riverside Restaurant, which still stands today, managed by Anne and Anthony Kelly. Next door was Bridget McKenzie, who was a dressmaker. Her neighbours were the Corley family and later on, the Kilroy sisters from Bellaghy. Pake

Devanney was next and his daughter Kitty is still with us. Next to them were the Campbells. They had a daughter Rose and a son Joe, who became a doctor but sadly died a young man.

Michael Carr's family was next. He had a barber shop and also ran a hackney service. James Healy and his wife Sadie operated a bar next to Michael Carr's. Jack Donoghue had a bakery beside Healy's, and it was still functioning up to the early 1970s, when they built new premises in Lowpark near Cruck Ruagh. Beside our house on the church side were Mary Gallagher and Bridie McGowan, who were dressmakers. Sharing the house with them were Annie and Tom Brennan. Tom was a general handyman and is still with us. Sadly Annie died many years ago, and I will always remember her for her wit and good humour.

Pa FitzMaurice and his brother Eddy ran a butcher shop for a while. Then Eddy left, married in Bellaghy and operated a drapery shop there for many years. Pa then opened a bar and carried on at that trade until the 1970s. The bar was very well frequented by my father and all the neighbours.

Tom Maloney and family lived next to the house which was known as Weaver's; it was empty when we were young. It was later bought by Vincent Doherty. Tom Maloney was involved in the dillisk and day-old-chicks trade. Later on his sons went into the hackney business. Then Kevin and his wife Mary had a dry-cleaning service, which is in operation to this day. Tom Maloney's grand-nephew, Fr Michael, is now our curate in Charlestown.

Other people that I remember were: Martin Horkan, who had a garage and also ran a hackney service for many years (his sons Marty and Collie are carrying on the trade); Patsy Gallagher, his wife May, their daughter Marie who was a nurse and their son John who is now a barrister in Dublin; Mike Doherty, whose son Vincent is now a Director of Dual Engineering in Lowpark, and the Morrisroe sisters, Fanny Morrisroe and Mrs McLoughlin, who were sisters of the late Jim Morrisroe, TD.

Paddy Casey ran a very successful bar and grocery. His wife was a National School teacher. Another house was occupied by Charlie Kelly and his sister Annie. 'Yes Boy' Durkin ran a bar and his wife was a teacher. Matt Cassidy and his wife were both teachers, and my father was best man at their wedding. Thomas Edward Henry was a plumber and his wife ran a pharmacy, which is still in business. Next to them, the house formerly occupied by

Johanna Kilroy and Teresa Jordan, *c.*1953.

the late John E. Doherty was owned by the nuns of the Marist order. Baby Tumour Gallagher and her brother ran a grocery shop. It was burned down in the 1960s. Nan Moffit owned a bar and ran a very successful business for many years.

The teachers I remember were Michael Francis Swords, Johnny Cassidy, Mrs Lucy Coleman and Sister Tomasina, all of whom taught in the Lowpark National School.

P.J. Henry and John McIntyre both operated mineral water bottling plants. I worked in both as a teenager. Great friends of my father were: Joe Finan, publican; Tom Durkin, publican and councillor; Pa FitzMaurice, publican; Michael Carr; Laddy Mulrooney, and Douglas Kelly, a solicitor who was best man at his wedding. Dad was a good golfer in his youth and was a member of Swinford Golf Club.

I have fond memories, too, of Mike Dillon of Main Street, Delia Sweeney of the Square and Mary Horkan and Teresa Cassidy who lived in Church Street. My cousins John, Michael and Siobhan Henry spent many summers with us in the 1940s. Michael and Brian Henry, sons of my uncle Mick also visited.

DELIA HENRY

My mother, Delia Henry, provided me with these snippets about Charlestown.

CURES

Good wholesome food produced on our own little farm was responsible for our healthy condition. My mother, who was an O'Donnell from Ardara, was doctor, baker, and dressmaker, all in one.

On one special event, I remember a doctor being called to our house. My brother fell off a donkey and injured his head, this necessitated a few stitches, and he made a full recovery. Of course there was the scourge of TB, which we escaped, but a pal of mine died of it when we were about eight years old. We owe a great deal of gratitude to Dr Noel Brown, who pioneered the treatment

The Killaturley National Band, *c*.1930.

Lenihan Family of Killaturley, *c.*1924. Back row, left to right: Mike, Mary, Ted, Annie, Johnny. Front, left to right: Winnie, John (father), Cathleen, Winnie *née* O'Donnell (mother), Paddy, Delia.

and eradication of this disease, which ravished the country for years. Now, with people having medical cards, giving free medical attention to the holders, it makes life less hazardous, which means a more content community.

Animals, too, got sick and died in the 1920s, before the Veterinary Surgeons came to our district. Prior to their advent, a man named Paddy Peter (Paddy McNicholas, from Cuilmore, Swinford), who was very well versed in animal ailments and diseases, did all he was capable of for the relief of the sick beasts, and with great success. Paddy was of medium build, lean and weather-beaten, like most country folk who do outdoor work. His knowledge of cattle illness was phenomenal. No house or barn was without a St Benedict's medal, which in those days was in great demand at the mission stalls when they came to the Parish. It could be said that between them, the Saint and Paddy worked wonders with the animals. Today with milking machines and parlours, the cows' kingdom has improved beyond our wildest imaginations, with injections for every malady. Hygienic surroundings are a necessity and must be adhered to, since we depend on them for the greater part of our food – and why not treat them well?

FRIENDS

Now, I would like to write about neighbours and friends. One very dear and important lady in our village was Maire Sheain, the wife of the local tailor, Frain. She was small in stature, rotund, but not overly stout, with snow-white hair, which was always shining and clean, and a nice apron over her dark clothes, that were in the the usual colour for married ladies. She was what was referred to then as 'stone deaf'.

She filled the important role of midwife for the area, until a local girl, Nurse Mulligan qualified in the late 1910s (the local area being Killaturley and Barnacogue). No one ever heard her complain of her hearing problem, which occurred in her middle age. She was always in good humour and full of fun and laughter. To put her point home she would poke the listener with her clean, fat hands.

Her house consisted of two rooms and like the 'Old woman of the Roads' she had a dresser full of shining delph, which she washed monthly. She also catered for a family. I remember seeing the tailor sitting cross-legged on the kitchen table, doing some hand sewing, and my delight at receiving the spools when the thread had been used. In our kitchen there was a line of spools on a wire from wall to wall on which clothes, when ironed, were laid across to air. This was of course long before the hot-press era.

LOCAL CUSTOMS

I would like to remind my readers that I was born in the year 1910 in Killaturley. At the side of the house were the usual barns. One barn, belonging to the tailor Frain had a good floor and a Dancing Master called Towey came here to teach Irish dancing when I was about eight years old. The younger members attended classes after school; the night time was for adults. It was autumn and I was on my way to the class one evening over the field where the oats were being cut, and I stopped to chat with the family working there. My mother, who happened to be there at the time, looked very critically at me and told me to come back home as I had measles. This malady lasted for some time, and by the time I'd recovered the dancing was over.

The social life for the adults then was limited to house dances, parties, weddings, and visitors to the home, as well as farewell dances for those going to America. The functions rotated, but when there was music in a house, it was often an opportunity to hold one. When a dance was to be held in our house, it was amazing to watch our older siblings lead up to the introduction of the idea. My parents had to be put in a receptive mood, especially my father. That was accomplished by them by being very diligent and agreeable where work was concerned, making refusal almost impossible. When the night came, we, the young ones, collected chairs from the nearby houses to seat the would-be dancers. By eight o'clock, with the milking done and the cattle fed, it was time to welcome the visitors. Soon the kitchen would be filled; the late arrivals would have to sit on people's knees.

The seating was important. In most old houses there was a place off the kitchen for a snugbed, about which were nice decorative curtains and a long chair by the outside. The more mature girls who had steady boyfriends would try to pick a seat by the bed for the purpose of using the curtain as a cover for them when they wanted a cuddle. As the music struck up, the dancing

Members of the Lenihan family, pictured in 1927. Left to right: Ted, Johnny, Mary.

began and continued with zest, diversifying with singing and step-dancing to supplement the set-dances. Towards the end of the revelry, a self-appointed matchmaker would start 'share the women', that is to be a go-between for people who liked each other, but were too shy to make advances. This very often started a romance that later blossomed into marriage.

I remember being taken out of bed on a night to dance a reel at our house dance. One had to be over seventeen to be allowed to a dance, as the adults did not relish young ones in their way, but we danced with our own age group. My cousin Martin Lenihan and our friend and neighbour Tom Rush were wonderful accordion players, much sought after for all occasions. Tom was my dancing partner, when he was not playing.

Then I went to college. By the time I was trained, Tom and Martin had joined the emigrant trail to America. Tom became a priest after a late vocation and did very good work. He came home on two occasions and when we met we relived some of the escapades of our youth. Then Fr Tom passed away to his eternal reward. His young brother Pete stayed at home. In the evenings he came for the white horse which he grazed in the field adjoining our land. Astride the animal as they wandered homeward across the river, he played jigs, reels and lovely Irish melodies on the wooden flute, which echoed over the low hills until it became a wandering sound. He too had to go.

PROGRESS

The way we spend our leisure time has certainly progressed, and our social lives have undergone many changes for the better. Radio – 'the thief of conversation' – was a big upheaval, coming into the homes slowly but surely. Where electricity had not yet reached, batteries were used. The radio had its advantages; the listener could hear the events being relayed to his own satisfaction without fear of contradiction, and he could be relaxed, unless he was listening to a football match.

The television came and almost took over the home. To interrupt a programme in company was almost a sin. Work was scheduled to fit in with the picture or saga, until such times as people became more selective in their viewing. Now it is part of the kitchen furniture, through which one can see the workings of the world, at peace or at war, prosperous or starving, happy or sad. It is progress, it is good; take the best it offers.

TED MCDONNELL

Ted McDonnell was born on 8 June 1916, in Lurga West, Charlestown, Co. Mayo. He was christened Edward Francis in Bushfield church. His father was Patrick 'Sean', and his mother was Anne, *née* Frain, from Kilgarriff. He came from a family of nine, a sister Rita died in 1923 aged nine. His other brothers and sisters were: James, born 1908; Martin, 1910; Jack, 1912; Michael, 1913; Bill, 1919; Catherine, 1909, and Bridget (Bee) in 1918.

Ted has very fond memories of his neighbours during the roaring twenties, including: Patrick Hopkins and his wife 'Sis' *née* Haran; Patrick Lavin, whose daughter Mary died tragically in a motor accident in Charlestown in the late 1930s; Thomas Frain, Kilgarriff, uncle of all the McDonnells; John McDonnell (no relation) and his wife Molly Tiernan of Lurga; Tom Hopkins; Pat Birmingham and his wife Nell Harrington, and Joe Dillon and Sean Morris of Lurga.

Going to School in Cloonlyon was a special treat for him. His teachers were John 'Cooper' Murphy, the Mulligan sisters, and Mrs Burke, who taught in the girls' section. Some of his classmates were Bill Sloyan, Jimmy 'Sam' Brennan, Dominick O'Donnell, Jack Keane, Mick Lenihan, Mick Cunnane, Tom, Jack and Jim Gallagher, and Dominick Harrison. He enjoyed the 'errand boy' job he got from Mr Murphy on many an occasion. He sent him many times to Bid 'Luke Sean' Cafferty's shop, near Bushfield church, to fetch the groceries for the school. This shop was later to become Mulligan's and was operated in later years by Willie and his wife Mary.

When thinking about the late twenties and early thirties, Ted has a long list of people that he likes to mention: Tony Haran; Andy Vesey; Pat 'Butty' Maye; Tom 'Alec' McDonnell; Tom, Jim and Bill McNulty; Jim and Johnny Birmingham; Martin and Lawrence Mulherne; Patrick and Anne Horkan; John and Kate Healy; Mick and Mary Kate Doherty, who for many years had a small grocery shop in Kilgarriff; H. Gallagher; Thomas Jordan; Henry Frain, and the famous handballer Mickey Walsh. As young boys they used to play on Croic na mBuacailli (The hill of the Boys), later called Dooney's Hill, which today is to your right as you enter Ireland West Airport. The other hill was Croic Eoghan in Hagfield. Ted continues his reminiscences:

> Some of the greatest pleasures I had while growing up was when working with my father. Whether it was saving the hay, working in the bog,

or going to the fair in Charlestown, it was all a wonderful. While making the 'reeks' of hay, I was always waiting for the order, 'Ted, go to town to Murray's Pub and bring back three jars of stout.' I saddled the donkey and off I went on my merry way. Boy, were the men delighted when I returned with my refreshments! The bog was situated where Ireland West Airport is now, and how things have advanced for the better.

Then we often went to the fair, with the mule and cart loaded with bon-hams to sell in town. I enjoyed the town, shopping in Mary Carroll's and buying the animal foods in Michael Gavaghan's in Bellaghy (who had strong connections in Kilgarriff).

My father had a famous horse called Teapot and often we set off with Teapot and cart, loaded with turf to sell at 7s a crib to Jim Webb, Mary Carroll, Murray's Pub, Paddy Gallagher, Martin Dunne, Annie Walsh and others. Teapot was often entered into the races at Tample pattern sports, which was held on 11 August each year. He was a great horse and won many a race.

Later on, my father sold Teapot to John McIntyre, mineral water manufacturer in Charlestown. Mr McIntyre watched the horse race in Tample and liked what he saw. He thought that he would be useful for delivering goods to his custom-ers, but he didn't know about his mood swings, and one day, while delivering in Swinford, Teapot had enough and he broke away, galloping all the way back to Charlestown. Needless to say, when Mr McIntyre returned home, he was not very pleased. He decided to sell the horse and duly did so at a fair in Castlerea. Teapot was bought as a cavalry horse by a representative for the British Army.

One of the famous characters that lived in Charlestown then was a man that everyone called Boss Gilbride. His real name was Dominick McBride, and he was a retired American Army officer. When he had a few drinks on receiving his pension, anything could happen, and often it did. Boss went to last Mass one Sunday, feeling the worse for wear. When he arrived in the church, an elderly gentleman, feeling the worse for smoking too many woodbines, could not stop coughing. Boss got annoyed, marched down to the unfortunate man, and issued the order, 'Go home and die, you son of a bitch!' Boss died in 1953, aged eighty-four years of age.

While still domiciled in Lurga West, my youthful days were spent enjoying life as best I could in that little world around me, going to Mass every Sunday in Bushfield church, meeting all the friends and neighbours, and of course listening to all the stories from people who had returned from far-away places. I had dreams too, like every young person around, of seeing the World, or at least part of it.

I remember fondly the priests who said Mass for us; Fr Denis Gildea, Fr Gallagher and Fr Kirwan. I got a little older, and my next adventure was attending the local dances and looking for the girl of my dreams. The reality would have to wait until many years later, when I travelled to America, but more of that later on.

The dance halls that I frequented were: Walsh's Central Ballroom, Charlestown; O'Donnell's Hall, Lavey; Murphy's Hall, Lecarrow; Lenihan's in Shammer; Dunleavy's in Tavrane; Haran's in Madogue, and last but not least, Tom Nell's Hall in Killaturley. From all around they came to those dances, and of course we danced well into the early hours of the following morning, many times returning home alone, and looking forward to the next encounter.

As they say, time moves on, and I had to move with the times and on to another place. That place was Lincolnshire. Michael Mulherne and myself got a bus outside Honan's in Charlestown and off we went on our journey through life. The year was 1935, the place Mr Richardson's farm, Morton Grove, Lincolnshire, England. The work consisted mostly of harvesting potatoes and beet pulling. I spent thirteen years in England altogether, ten years on the farm, and three years in Coventry. There was a lot of work in and around Coventry, as the Germans had bombed the city very heavily. I spent three years there, from 1945 to 1948, and I remember well the following men that worked there with me: Andy Vesey; Mairteen Mulligan; Mick and Jack Frain; the McNulty brothers, and Dooney brothers.

I returned home in 1948, mostly to spend some time with my parents, and to prepare for my departure to America. It was a lonely time for me, mainly because I knew that it was much easier to visit home from England than it would be from America. But I was determined to go and off I went, purchasing my ticket from Joe P.A. Mulligan, shipping agent. I set sail from Cobh in Cork on 18 June 1948 and arrived in New York on 26 June. I was claimed by Mike Hopkins, brother of Patrick Hopkins, Lurga.

A grand old lady of Hackfield, Liz Keane, gave me a farewell message, 'Ted, do not forget to visit your uncle, Jim McDonnell in Philadelphia.' My uncle Jim was eighty-two years of age at the time and still working as a steel tester. I stayed with him for two days and then I was off to Chicago.

When I arrived in Chicago, I was met by my brothers Jim and Martin, and sisters Catherine and Bridget. I stayed with Jim for a good spell at his home in 2204 Wilson Avenue. Two of my greatest friends during my long stay in Chicago were Pat Brennan and Tom Carroll, who both worked with the Chicago Transport Authority (CTA). Tom Carroll was married to my sister Catherine and Pat Brennan was married to Tom Carroll's sister Delia.

I commenced work with the CTA on 6 July 1948 as a bus serviceman. I lived for a while with my brother Martin, who resided at South Hoyne Avenue. The depot where I worked was at Archer Avenue. Slowly I improved my position with the company, graduating to repairs and maintenance. In the evenings, when I finished at CTA, I did some part-time work at Marshall Field's Clothing store. I then transferred to the Motor Coach Company in Keeler Avenue. That company was owned by CTA. This job was close to my new home at 29-46 North Kenneth. I stayed with CTA for most of my working life.

Now, to the girl of my dreams, Agnes 'Sis' Horkan, from Kilgarriff. We got married in 1952 and my best man was Tom Higgins and the bridesmaid was Vera Horkan. I had a lovely married life with a wonderful wife and family. Patricia was born in 1953 and still lives in Chicago with her husband Tony and children, Britney, Taylor and Bailey. Eddy was born in 1954, and now lives in Arizona with his wife Laura. Finally, Joyce was born in 1956.

My loving wife Agnes died in 1995 and is buried in Maryhill Cemetery. I sold my house at North Kenneth in 1998 and bought a condo at Linder and Lawrence in 1999. My granddaughter Megan still lives in Chicago, and my other granddaughter Kelsey lives in Barnacogue with Joyce and Tom Sweeney.

While in Chicago I was a member of the Shamrock American Club and the Irish American Heritage Society in North Knox. Some bars that I frequented were Emmett's at Milwaukee and Grand Avenue, Jimmy Lynch's Bar, and Galvin's and Ryan's at Western Avenue. I had a lot of time to visit these taverns when I retired in 1981.

The following words are written of Ted McDonnell:

What else could he have been born for – he took his chances. With his bright heart he gave his greatest gifts to his family with a smile of satisfaction having lived a full and wonderful life. After all, he had something to give which was of great value to them.

He followed the path that took him from Lurga West to Charlestown, then on to Lincolnshire and Coventry in England, home again, saying a fond farewell to his loving parents, travelling on to America, and finally returning to Barnacogue, to his loving daughter Joyce and son-in-law Tom.

What could he do but smile.

TALES OF MY FATHER

The following pieces about Charlestown were relayed to me by my father, Tony Henry (1900-1982).

ALEC MCCABE

Alec McCabe and Mr Brady of Ballymote were on hunger strike in Sligo Jail in the year 1917/1918. I was going to Summerhill College at the time and my pal was J. Keane, whose father was Governor of Sligo Jail. There was a ball court in the jail and my pal and I often went in for a game. On one occasion we were passing by a cell and Alec McCabe called me and said, 'Hello Tony, get me some cigarettes.' I told my aunt Mrs McDonagh and the next day she gave me the cigarettes. We went for a game of hand-ball and when I got the opportunity I gave Mr McCabe the cigarettes, not letting my pal see me. He thanked me very much afterwards. After Mr McCabe's release from jail, he was elected a TD for Sligo–Leitrim and later on founded the Educational Building Society in Dublin.

On the day the truce between the British and Irish was signed, Captain Marren of the old IRA, a native of Ballymote, was drowned in Strandhill. Matt Brennan and I went to the funeral. The firing party consisted of Alec McCabe, Jim Hunt, Joe Finnegan and B. Brady. When all was over we came home and Matt went into our bar for a drink. In the bar were Captain Harte and Lt Leyrode.

Leyrode was a small man, Harte a big man, and Matt Brennan was telling them about all the Black and Tans he shot. My mother, who was formerly Margaret Filan, heard the loud talk and called Matt out to see if he had a gun. She would not let him back in. Lt Leyrode said, 'I will search him if he comes back in.' I said, 'You will not while I am here.' I brought Leyrode outside and put him on the ground. 'Good man Tony,' said Captain Harte, 'he cannot search him because the truce is still on.'

THE RAILWAY LINE

Around the year 1892 the Claremorris and Swinford Unions appointed James McGarry, Conor O'Kelly, Tommy Kelly and my father Mark Henry, to meet with the British Prime Minister Mr Bonar Law, to convince the Government of the day to run the railway line from Claremorris through Swinford and Charlestown to Colloney in Sligo. As we now know, they succeeded.

The first Station Master was a Mr Broderick; the last Station Master was a Mr Currid. Bill Henderson was the original signalman. The first passenger train to run through Charlestown was on the first Wednesday of February, 1895, driven by a Mr Jones. The last train to run was in October 1975. The driver that day was Mr James O'Grady and the guard was Mr Paddy Bree from Sligo.

BUSHFIELD CHURCH

On one occasion my wife Delia and I were discussing Bushfield church, and when it may have been built. Delia spoke to her cousin Mike Lenehan of Kileen and asked him to talk to Thomas Durkan, his neighbour. Thomas was then eighty-two years old. He said that he was in Bushfield church in 1912 on the day Fr T.P. Gallagher came to say his first Mass, having been appointed curate in Charlestown Parish.

Fr Gallagher said to some men who were standing outside the church, 'You have a very nice church here, can you tell me what year it was built?' A man named Peter Higgins from Killeen spoke up and said, 'Twenty-five years ago.' This would mean that Bushfield church was built in 1887.

JOHN HARDIMAN

The first solicitor in Charlestown was Mr John Hardiman, a Limerick man and a relation of the family who owned the *Limerick Leader*. In September 1915, the Charlestown AOH had a meeting to raise funds for the widow and orphans of the late John Hardiman. The family had fallen on hard times through no fault of their own. The treasurers of that fundraising committee were: Mr J. Howley, solicitor, Tubbercurry; Mr P. O'Connor, solicitor, Swinford; Mr R. Fitzmaurice, Hibernian Bank, Tubbercurry, and Mr M.C. Henry, Charlestown. Hardiman's son Willie later moved to Florida and died there some years ago.

RENT FREE

My great-grandfather John Mulligan, whose wife was Elizabeth Haran, built the first house in Charlestown in 1846 for his soon-to-be-married daughter Mary. She married Michael Henry from Swinford and set up shop in the new town. Many years later their son Mark got a bill for £60 for rent from Loughlynn House, where Charles Strickland lived. Mark asked what the bill was for, as he was told that the house was rent free forever. Mark duly went to Loughlynn and met Charles Strickland and Sir Henry Doran. My father said he could not pay all of the £60. 'So,' said Henry Doran, 'give me £5.' My father paid the £5 and of course the house became rent free forever.

ELECTRICITY

The Charlestown Electric Light and Power Co. Ltd was set up by Canon Keveney in the early 1900s. It is said that Charlestown was the first town in the west to generate its own electricity. The following receipts will show the cost of electricity at that time:

> Received from Canon Keveney: 5s 4d for sixteen units at 4d a unit,
> M.C. Henry: £1 5s for seventy-five units at 4d a unit,
> P.A. Mulligan: 9s for twenty-seven units at 4d a unit,
> J.J. Murray: 5s 4d for sixteen units at 4d a unit.
>
> All receipts were for the month of September 1911.

The power station was situated where the Health Centre now stands. Michael Brennan was the Station Manager. The authorised collector for the company was the father of the late Andy Vesey of Tavneena.

CHARLESTOWN FEIS

The Achonry Diocesan Feis was held in Charlestown on 23-24 August 1904. The patron was Most Revd J. Lester, Lord Bishop of Achonry, and the committee comprised:

> President: Revd M. Keveney, PP
> Vice-presidents: Revd P. Mulligan, PP, Curry; Mr M.J. O'Doherty, NT; Revd
>   J. Daly Ballaghaderreen.
> Treasurers: M.C. Henry; D. Marren, Swinford; Revd J. Spellman, Kilmactigue.
> Secretaries: Revd M. Devine, CC; Mr J.E. O'Doherty, Charlestown.

THE BALL ALLEY

The old ball alley, or handball court, was situated behind what is now the Fire Brigade headquarters near the Town Hall. The handball court was opened on 31 May 1931 by Dr Morrisroe, Bishop of Achonry, who hailed from Charlestown. It cost over £300 to build and it complied with all the regulations for championship matches.

The committee responsible for making it happen were:

Patron: Revd C. Gildea, PP.
President: Revd Denis Gildea, CC.
Vice-president: Jim Morrisroe.
Treasurers: P.J. Honan, Willie Moffitt.
Secretaries: Tony Henry, Bernie Cassidy.
General Manager: Paddy Brennan.
General Committee: James Parsons, P. Collins, Luke Colleran and Leo Cahill.

The ball court was built by the Regan family of Barrack Street.

VALUE FOR MONEY

My grandmother Mulligan had four or five neighbours helping with the hay in her land in Ballyglass one summer's day in the year 1887. One of the men was Dick McGowan. His little son, then aged about seven or eight, was in the field with them. My grandmother went up to the fields with a drink for the men, wearing a white bonnet and apron. She called young McGowan and asked him his name. He said, 'Jim McGowan Ma'am.' 'Are you Dick's son?' she asked. He said he was. She put her hand in her apron pocket to see if she

The Charlestown Pipe Band c.1930, including: Pat Brennan, Master; Tom Brennan, uile-ann pipes; Mike Doherty, big bass drum; Pete Brennan, and Mr Foley of Barrack Street.

Above left: Most Revd Dr Morrisroe, Bishop of Achonry, being presented with a basket of flowers by Teresa and Maureen Brennan on his arrival at St James's church for their first holy communion, 6 August 1936.

Above right: Most Revd Dr Morrisroe, Bishop of Achonry, who visited his native Charlestown on the occasion of his Episcopal Silver Jubilee, August 1936. He is photographed here with members of the reception Committee: Tony Henry, Luke Mulligan, J. Cassidy NT, P. Campbell, J. Mulrooney, V. Harrison, B. Campbell, M. Brennan.

had a halfpenny or a penny. All she had was a shilling. She gave it to young Jim. His father called him and asked his son why she gave him the money. Jim said that she would not take it back. Dick McGowan told him to go down to the town and get two ounces of tobacco, one loaf of bread, one pint of lamp oil, and a halfpenny worth of sweets. Well young Jim did that and when he came back up, he had one penny and a halfpenny left from the shilling.

TOM AND MOLLY

When I first got to know Tom Carroll, he was probably in his early thirties, just after the Second World War. He was CIE's official carter from the railway station in Charlestown. The entire economy of the town depended on him and his faithful brown mare, Molly. They delivered all the articles from the goods store on time, in an open-sided cart, with large steel-clad wooden wheels. Tom was always dressed in blue overalls, heavy serge pants, hobnailed boots, a dark blue shirt and a battered tweed cap. Only in really severe weather did he use a heavy black coat. Living about a mile outside the town, he was of small, light stature but boy could he handle a bag of sugar, a large chest of tea or a long side of bacon! He also dropped heavy timber Guinness firkins on to a cork-filled canvas bag.

He collected Molly and started work at noon. Then he went through the notes pinned for him on the station's large store door by frantic businessmen, eagerly awaiting their bags of cement, boxes of bearings, lengths of piping, etc. These shopkeepers had to tell early morning customers that their requirement was at the station and they would have to await Tom's arrival. He saw to it that those 'emergency calls' were dealt with first. His very pleasing, ever-helpful personality and trustworthy reputation endeared him to everyone.

Above left: The well-known distillers John Power & Son and John Jameson & Sons Ltd supplied whiskey and printed labels to local merchants. Regular checks were carried out to make sure that the whiskey was properly bottled for sale to customers.

Above right: 'O'Connell's Pale Ale' label. Ale was supplied in barrels and half-barrels by such well-known companies as Arthur Guinness, Smithwicks, McArdle Moore, O'Connells and George Younger. The ale was transported to Ballaghaderreen by the Midland Great Western Railway Company. It was then collected by a carter and brought to Charlestown.

Molly was affectionately looked after; her well-brushed coat a tes-
timony to this fact. A nosebag of oats was always available to her, her
harness was of the best quality, and she was well shod at all times. In the
summer evenings as Tom led Molly out to her field, he would often give
some local children a ride on her. Only once ever did I see her 'fall on the
job'. She was drawing a well-laden cart of beers and minerals from our
wholesale premises, for Tom to convey to local customers during a frosty
Christmas week. Suddenly she slipped and fell. In her panic she broke her
harness and sped away down the street, with Tom, still holding on to the
reins, in hot pursuit. He eventually stopped her on the outskirts of the
town, both of them totally exhausted. The debris of broken bottles from
the overturned cart, having created a major traffic jam in the street, was
finally cleared up by a meitheal of neighbours armed with brushes and
shovels, and deposited into empty barrels. Molly's only holiday from work
was during the weeks leading up to her confinements. Tom would then
obtain a replacement from his friend Charlie Ward, who generally kept a
few horses around his encampment for his own transport. From time to
time you would see the attractive sight of a young foal trotting alongside
Molly on her rounds.

We received Guinness stout in fifty-two-gallon hogsheads, which Tom
would deliver to us three at a time (a very wobbly load), to be bottled for
distribution to other towns. When he arrived at our store entrance he would
back his cart into two ruts in the ground which we had dug for him. This
enabled him to bring his cart down to the axle, in order to have the load at
ground level. The wooden barrels were then rolled off very easily. He occa-
sionally delivered orders around the town for us, writing out the invoices
and collecting the money as well. It was all cash on delivery in those days
and he would drop into our office the following morning, pockets bulging
with pounds.

Throughout the big snow of 1947, when all transport was at a standstill,
he had a rough manner of sleigh built for Molly. With this contraption, he
managed to get fowl, vegetables, churns of milk, creels of turf and even
cocks of hay brought to the townspeople from the local farms. My abiding recollection of those few isolated weeks was seeing this heroic duo and
the sleigh passing our house with a coffin for burial in the local cemetery.
They were accompanied by a large group of walking mourners, trudging
knee-deep through the snow. Tom, conscious of his reverential undertaking,

wore his best black suit, tie and white shirt and Molly had her brass-studded harness gleaming in the frosty air.

During the early fifties a pre-Christmas pantomime was being staged in the town. It was decided, as an opening treat before the Sunday matinee, that Santa would arrive at the railway platform to be greeted by all the children of the area. With the co-operation of the station master, who was in the show, our Father Christmas was placed on a maintenance buggy on the tracks about a mile outside the town, near the top of the hill and loaded with goodies. It was then let run down the incline right into the station, accompanied by fireworks, which had been placed along the line. Welcoming him on arrival was our Mayor, wearing a dozen flattened crown caps as his chain of office. Outside the station waited a glittering golden 'coach and one'. This consisted of a heavily camouflaged Tom, Molly and cart. The effect was indeed regal. Timber beer cases turned upside down and covered in multi-coloured Christmas paper, with drapes of golden tinsel all around the sides, provided the dais. A red painted tea chest served as Santa's seat, surrounded by balloons of various hues. With flagpoles at each end covered in holly, and crepe paper wrapped around the wheel spokes and shafts, it was certainly a carriage fit for Father Christmas.

For Molly it was her moment of glory. She stood like an Arab steed, her body festooned with dozens of Christmas lights and seasonal decorations, bells, angels, stars, and of course silver horseshoes for luck. Over her nostrils she wore a large bulbous, flaming red nose à la Rudolph. But the pièce de résistance was the set of antlers on her ears.

Fitted out, not too comfortably, in a Dickensian coachman's costume was Tom himself, complete with top hat and whip. What an overall spectacle it was, with Santa was ensconced on his 'throne', being escorted through the town. Every street had to be visited on the way to the Town Hall. He was cheered on by hundreds of mesmerised children, who will no doubt remember forever Santa's first magical visit to their own place.

In his social life, Tom had two passions. One was dancing. Being a non-driver he always booked a hackney car for the out-of-town venues and would bring a few of his friends with him wherever the top bands of the day were playing. Bert Flynn, Stephen Garvey and Brose Walsh were the big drawing cards. My first away trip with his group was to the newly opened Astor Ballroom in Roscommon. We were all fascinated, watching the new-fangled Crystal Ball spinning from the ceiling as it turned the place into a kaleidoscope of colour. The era of the modern ballroom had arrived. Tom may not have actually danced very much but he loved the music, the crowds and the whole atmosphere.

His other lifelong interest was gambling, or more specifically 'pitch and toss'. The side of the handball alley was the most popular venue and there the crowds would gather in the summer evenings. The game consisted of placing two pennies on a comb and tossing them up in the air. Tom always acted as banker and because he bet on the two coins turning up 'harps' when they hit the ground, everybody else hoped their heavily supported 'heads' would show up.

Through all weathers and into the night, under candlelight or hand-held

This photograph was taken in the old Town Hall, Charlestown in 1954, prior to the performance of *Cinderella*. Back row, left to right: Mick Higgins, Tommy Doohan, Mick Mulligan, Sean Tiernan, Tommy Jordan, Gerry Healy, Sean Honan, Frank Connerton, John Mahon, G. Walsh. Second row, left to right: Mary Frain, Bernadette Cassidy, Meta Mahon, Breege Murphy, Cathleen Dunleavy, May Honan. Third row, left to right: Helen Carr, Ita Carr, Mary Jo McIntyre, Veronica Henry, Olive Gallagher, Eamonn O'Hara, Mary Margaret Marren, Bridgie Duffy, Francie Walsh, Mrs Rafferty (pianist), Tommy Moffitt. Fourth row: Mickey Frain (George), Paddy Henry, Seamie Fleming, Joe Logue, Bill Doran, Mickey Frain.

● Young dancers in the show include, Kathleen Blake, Rosaleen Blythe, Pauline Mahon, Ann Harrison, Attracta Moffat, Imelda Cassidy, Patricia Mulligan, Finola Bermingham, Bridget Brennan, Maureen Mulligan, Peg Egan.

The cast of *Cinderella*, 1956. The dancers pictured include Kathleen Blake, Rosaleen Blythe, Pauline Mahon, Ann Harrison, Attracta Moffat, Imelda Cassidy, Patricia Mulligan, Finola Bermingham, Bridget Brennan, Maureen Mulligan, Peg Egan. Mary Margaret Marren who played Cinderella is pictured on the bottom left.

torch, Tom continued taking bets, squatted down on his hunkers. On very wet evenings he and his entourage of about twelve would adjourn to Jim Terry's forge and play by the eerie light of the constantly bellowed furnace, with the sound of the rain drumming down on the galvanised roof. With the arrival of extended public street lighting they moved to the brighter light at the gable end of an old disused dance hall and operated there for many years. No one knew how Tom fared financially at his gambling, but he was never short and always laid his bets in cash. During the long bank closure in 1970, he was always able to change the wage or milk cheques for his associates and must have had a very large lodgement to make when the strike was over.

As the years went by and companies began to use their own road transport, Tom's days were numbered. Rail traffic declined dramatically and he was eventually reduced to a donkey and cart for the few meagre deliveries. Molly was no longer required and he was anxious to find a good home for her. One day he answered a box-number advertisement in the local paper,

'Horse required for light work around extensive farm. Good home assured.'
He duly met the farm manager involved who convinced him Molly would
be well looked after. So he sent her off in a horse box and jeep to her
new dwelling place in a village called Classiebawn in Co. Sligo. About three
months afterwards he got a rather formal letter inviting him to come and
see Molly at work. It was signed 'Louis Mountbatten'.

Not a bit fazed, Tom asked me to drive him there. We arrived on the
requested date and he was delighted to see Molly looking so well. He had a
short conversation with 'the Lord' (as he called him). They talked about various
aspects of horseflesh, their breeding, harness requirements, feeding habits and
the skills involved in breaking them in. Tom was in his element. On the way
home he was very quiet and eventually I asked him how he felt. After a short
pause he said, 'Did you see the tears in Molly's eyes when we were leaving?'

His working term with his donkey and cart was short lived, as our branch
line closed down after about two years due to reduced use. One incident
stands out in my mind from those declining days. In the early seventies our
local bank was being merged into a larger group and the switch over to
new stationery and logo was set to start nationwide at 10a.m. on a particular
day. By then all branches would have received the new paperwork. When
the consignment had not arrived by opening time, the distraught manager
sent out an SOS for Tom. He couldn't be found. As he had the keys of the

Charlestown fancy dress ball, 1951. The caption reads, 'Only a colour film could do
justice to the variety of hue and design in the costumes.'

station store with him, nothing could be done until his arrival. Eventually, at ten past twelve, Tom, on his reduced four-footed delivery vehicle, arrived at the bank door. A stressed-out team of employees rushed to get the material from him. This was how our town belatedly entered the electronic banking age, compliments of Tom.

Tom is long gone from us. His rail lifeline is now overgrown and silent, discos and nightclubs have replaced the dancehalls, and we now gamble on lotteries and televised sports events. The Mollys of old have virtually disappeared from our countryside. Yet the memories of those simple, carefree days will live on in our recollections of the Toms of this world. They were lovely, endearing people who earned our respect and affection by the total dedication they brought to their work and community.

Paddy Henry

HOME FROM THE USA

PATRICK KINSEY

After forty-nine years absence, a Charlestown patrolman based in Chicago visited home. The year was 1949 and that man was Patrick Kinsey, a brother of Brigid Kinsey (McKinsey) of Church Street who was a dressmaker. He had a very colourful life as an American cop. The following extract is from a *Western People* interview with the visiting Mr Kinsey:

> Standing six feet three inches tall and of a powerful build, he is accompanied by his wife, Mrs Agnes Kinsey, formerly Agnes Gallagher of Lurga, and a sister of Mrs Kilcoyne, Lurga. During the interview our correspondent asked him what his most thrilling experience was. He replied good-humouredly, 'Well I married a local girl.' He is the proud father of a family who seem to be bent on upholding justice in the USA – he has two sons in the police department, one son a lawyer, and a son-in-law also in the police force. All have seen active service with the US forces, serving on the continent, as well as in Manila and Japan. When further questioned about his experiences as a patrolman, he was very reluctant to discuss his activities, as he seemed to be still adhering to the rule that the police force must not give the press anything.

His wife, however, reminded him of a few incidents, one of which was about apprehending a burglar who had broken into a pork shop and was making his getaway down an alley before Patrolman Kinsey came on the scene. As the burglar failed to stop when called upon, Mr Kinsey drew his gun, fired, and dropped the burglar in his tracks with a leg wound. He had a side of bacon under his arm, and was … an Irishman.

Again he refused to be drawn out and he gave the reason why. He did not wish to hurt the feelings of burglars or their relatives by divulging anything about their lives, which might be put in the *Western People*, because, he added, 'when our fellows get the *Western* over there, everybody over there with a drop of Irish blood reads it from top to bottom, and then we pass it on, and I would not embarrass anyone'. His wife added, 'Anyway, he is one of those that never made many arrests.' When asked what the worst type of criminal was, and the most dangerous, the immediate reply was 'the Italians'. The beat had to be doubled in the Italian Quarter of Chicago and frequent shootings were due to feuds, which had started in Italy years ago, members of the Mafia society being particularly bitter and callous. Asked if he ever came in contact with Capone, he replied quite casually, that he had, several times. On one occasion he was assigned to visit Capone's house and was met by Capone's wife at the door. After a few formal questions were asked and answered, Mrs Capone offered him a drink saying, 'I suppose you would run me if I offered you a drink?' The reply was in the negative and he was seated in the parlour and was offered a beer and a double shot of brandy. Capone's mother hurried downstairs with a wealth of spaghetti and the leg of a chicken. 'Very nice people', he commented.

He explained about the great working of the vast forces of the FBI and the methods used to combat crime. The Irish Garda Síochána were, in his estimation, having a swell time with a lot less work to do. They carried themselves very well and with a good military bearing. This was very true of the Charlestown Guards, and, he concluded, all of them very good-looking men.

MR PATRICK BLAKE

In April 1949, Mr Patrick Blake was another Charlestown man to return home for a holiday, after twenty-two years in America. He lived in Long Island, New York, and was a carpenter by profession, working in the Todd shipyard in Brooklyn. Pat served in the repair of ships such as the *Brooklyn*, *Destroyer*, *Philadelphia*, *Washington*, and *Manhattan*. The *Western People* profiled him during his visit home. The clean-cut, well-spoken gentleman would have been better known to American radio fans as the host of 'Paddy Blake and his Irish Americans'. Pat broadcasted regularly over the American network, conducting the seven-piece Irish-American dance band, playing Irish songs only. Mr Blake was by that time an American citizen, but he said, 'My heart is here in Ireland.' He was married to an Irish girl, formerly May O'Shea, from Tipperary. He had two sons and one daughter. His elder son was a commercial artist while the younger one was a photographer. His daughter entered the Church. Pat was once a *Western People* newsboy and proud of it and told the newspaper that he was often disappointed when he could not get a copy in the international news agencies of Times Square.

When the reporter questioned him as to Harry Truman's unexpected win in the American Presidential election, he attributed it to overconfidence on the part of the Republican supporters who stayed away. Another reason was that the people dreaded a recurrence of the '29 slump. Pat voted for Mr Dewey, although he was a Democrat since he went to America, because Truman turned a deaf ear to the deputation sent by the Irish Republican Party for Truman's intercession in the border question back home. He predicted that Dewey would be elected next time and that Mayor O'Dwyer would go back again for another term in office. Regarding the Irish situation, Pat said that in Ireland they should not take a Republic for the twenty-six counties; it should be all or none.

According to the newspaper, Pat enjoyed his stay in Charlestown and had his accordion with him. He was a brother of Martin Blake, better known as 'Son', who was a drummer, crooner and accordionist in Wimsey's band, Tubbercurry. During his holiday he stayed with his mother in Barrack Street, Charlestown. In the late 1970s he retired to his home place and died here.

CATHERINE DURKAN AND THE *TITANIC*

Catherine Durkan (née McCormack) was interviewed by the late journalist Mick O'Connell for the Western People *in 1977.*

One of the nicest people it has ever been my pleasure to talk to comes from Ardara, near Charlestown. In her eighty-sixth year, she is Mrs Catherine Durkan, formerly Catherine McCormack. She has a vivid recollection of many happy episodes and one harrowing experience in her long and eventful life.

Catherine, or Katie as she is affectionately known, was attending Lowpark

National School in or around the year 1904 on the occasion of the County Feis in Charlestown, which was attended by many Irish scholars including Dr Douglas Hyde, who later became the first President of Ireland.

A special Irish competition in conjunction with the feis was held in the schools throughout the Diocese of Achonry. Katie takes great pride in the fact that she was the first prize winner in the competition. She says she received her prize of £10, a lot of money in those days, from the hands of Dr Hyde himself, who at that time was spearheading the Irish revival movement. She remembers Dr Hyde congratulating her and speaking to her in Irish. Katie was proficient in Irish because her father John McCormack and her grandmother were fluent Irish speakers. She says her father was also a great singer, shades of his famous namesake.

Katie went on to relate that her teachers in Lowpark at that time included, Mr and Mrs John E. Doherty. Mrs Doherty was trained in Paris and prepared a number of school choirs which won prizes at several Feiseanna. She recalled that the feis she referred to was not confined to music, singing and dancing competitions but also contained a section of the display of ancient Irish crafts, and there were also competitions in butter-making, basket-weaving, etc.

Katie travelled to America with her sister Mary on the *Carmania* in 1912, and later on she recalls that journey:

> I was a passenger on the *Carmania*, which was the first and only vessel to arrive at the scene of the disaster. The hour was around midnight and we all had retired for the night. Suddenly we heard a great commotion and people were rushing around outside. We went up on deck to see members of the crew lined along the railing of the vessel, standing shoulder to shoulder, and all of them were armed. We were not allowed near the railings. I could see from my position people who had tried to escape from the ill-fated *Titanic*, floundering in the water, which was calm. The lifeboats went out rescuing people as they came upon them. The *Titanic*, which had listed over, was close by and was slowly sinking out of sight. We returned to our sleeping quarters and prayed for all the passengers of the *Titanic* who were lost.

Katie described the witnessing of the disaster as a terrible, heartbreaking experience. She added, 'That night was the saddest night of my life. I still cry about it to this day.'

Mrs Katie Durkan is a lively and alert woman for her years. She is all her life a regular reader of the *Western People* and would not be without her weekly copy. She had five sisters and two brothers, and two sisters still survive, Mrs Ellen Ruane and Mrs Mary Healy in New York. Talking to her was a pleasure and it is our fervent wish that she will enjoy health and happiness for many years to come.

EMIGRANT REFLECTIONS

Many stories are written about emigration and their effects on the local community. Mostly they are sad tales of hardship, poverty and journeys into the unknown. Young people of today's Ireland do not understand how hard it was to exist back in the 1950s and 1960s. After they finished National School, most boys and girls had to go to the United States or Britain to find work. Those lucky enough to have secondary or vocational education might be able to find work in Ireland, otherwise they too would have to emigrate. All the doors that are open to the youth of today were not open then. It was very difficult for the young, but it was an even more sad and harrowing experience for their parents. One such couple were Jack and Mary Duffy (*née* Halligan) from Madogue near Charlestown. The following is a short account of two members of their family, namely Margaret and Paddy.

Margaret emigrated in 1962 and studied very hard in America. She graduated *magna cum laude* from Fordham University with a BS in accounting. She joined Arthur Andersen in 1972, and was admitted to the partnership in 1981. Arthur Anderson is one of the leading providers of accounting services. She was the first female audit partner of that firm. The company employs more than 62,000 people in seventy-two countries, including Ireland. Margaret was responsible for audit and business advisory services to major multi-national clients in numerous industries, ranging from consumer products to advertising. She is married to Eugene Gaughan and was a member of the Taoiseach's Ireland–America Economic Advisory Board and the American Ireland Fund, New York Dinner Committee.

Paddy Duffy's story of his leaving home is one that many other young people experienced, and he tells it very well:

7 August 1957. A date indelibly imprinted on my mind, the date I left home to go to the farmers in England. My belongings were packed; all my worldly possessions were in one suitcase with plenty of space to spare. A good fried breakfast was prepared by my mother, who kept encouraging me to eat plenty as I might not get another opportunity to eat before I got to Dublin. Soon it was time to go and catch the bus at the 'half-way-bush', a well-known locally recognised bus stop, approximately a half mile from my home.

My Dad had preceded me to the bus stop, my suitcase across his bicycle. There was the customary handshake with my brothers and sisters, a kiss from my tearful mother, and then it was time to walk the half-mile to the bus stop. My many neighbours came out to bid me farewell and placed some silver coins into my hand as 'Luck Money'.

On arriving at the half-way-bush where my Dad was waiting, I hoped that the bus would be late. I needed more time with him, but alas, within minutes, the bus came into view. So with a quick handshake, an embrace, and tears in our eyes, we said goodbye. I was on my way to England with three £5 notes in my newly acquired wallet and a pocketful of 'Luck Money' in half-crowns and two-shilling pieces. I glanced with nostalgia into the playground of Corthoon School, where I had spent ten happy carefree years, Sonnagh River where I had poached many fine salmon, and Sonnagh Road, where I did my first spot of courting. Very soon we were leaving Charlestown behind and on towards Dublin. I was now travelling through strange country, though less than twenty miles from home. I thought how small my world had been until that moment and I felt alone and insecure.

Paddy was on his way, and eventually he arrived in England. Some of the people he met there were of great help to the new emigrant, including Tom, Jim and Frank Burns, Tom McIntyre and Paddy Goldrick. Later on he met his cousins John and Paddy, and also Hughie Higgins from Killeen, and John Harrington from Carn. After some months his uncle John helped him find work with Grant Lyon. He was a general foreman with the company. That particular job had both civil and railway engineering content, since it involved the rebuilding of the quayside on the Manchester ship canal docks. Paddy acquired a good knowledge and the technical skills to undertake many tasks with a minimum of supervision. In 1964 he was given his first management position as Area Manager of the Midlands. By 1980 he was in the position of Regional Manager. This involved handling many high-profile projects. It was the era of the building of numerous railway systems, such as the Docklands Light Railway in east London, the Channel Tunnel, and many major city centre metro systems.

In December 1990, Grant Lyon was bought out by the powerful PLC British Steel. Paddy was invited to take over the position of UK Contracts Manager with a responsibility for all the UK sites. He was the first Irish person to hold this position in the history of the company. Paddy is now enjoying a happy retirement, a proud man in the knowledge of his achievements and a credit to his once tearful parents, Jack and Mary.

The Fourth Annual National Rosebud Final, which was held in Rolestown, Dublin, on 23 September 1962. Front row, left to right: Cork, Kildare, Kerry, Meath, Violet Collins of 'Mannequin', Armagh, Louth, Wicklow, Mayo. Back row, left to right: Cavan, Tyrone, Donegal, Derry, Jim Donoghue, Fermanagh, Wicklow, Wexford (the winning contestant).

JOHN HENRY

Professor John Henry, who died on 8 May 2007, aged sixty-eight years, was one of the world's leading authorities on drugs and poisons; his frequent appearances on television and radio made him Britain's best-known toxicologist and after his retirement in 2004 he continued to work as a medical expert, sought after around the world.

When, in September 2004, the Ukranian opposition leader Viktor Yushchenko fell seriously and mysteriously ill during the election campaign, Henry was sent a photograph of the patient and immediately concluded, due to the characteristic pattern of acne, that Yushchenko had been poisoned by dioxin. This had been missed by the doctors who had examined Yuschenko in Vienna, but a month later they confirmed the diagnosis. Henry was also called in as an advisor in the more recent cases of the former KGB agent Alexander Litvinenko and Pakistan cricket coach Bob Woolmer.

As professor of accident and emergency medicine at Imperial College, London, Henry broke new ground in the management of poisoning and drug overdose, helping to save the lives of many patients. He was also honorary consultant in accident and emergency medicine at St Mary's, Paddington, and visiting professor to the Radcliffe Infirmary, Oxford. Having suffered as a patient on dialysis for more than seven years, he exhibited great compassion to all the patients in his care. In 1982 he was appointed consultant physician at the National Poisons Unit at Guy's Hospital, where he saved a great many lives, particularly those of children who had accidentally ingested potentially lethal household products. He carried out research into how poisons worked and how they could be counteracted.

Henry had the ability to explain complex medical matters in simple terms and had an encyclopaedic knowledge of drugs and poisons. A typical story is of the occasion when he was in the resuscitation room attending a patient suffering from a drug overdose. When a colleague asked Henry why the patient's urine was green in colour, he immediately replied that the patient had obviously taken the drug Rohypnol. Tests proved this to be so.

He was especially concerned about the devastation wrought on young lives by illegal drugs. He insisted that cannabis was much more dangerous than simple tobacco and also explained how Ecstasy and amphetamines could cause death through hyperpyrexia and dehydration. He was one of the first to warn that the risks of taking Ecstasy had been underestimated and such were his vivid descriptions of the results of nightclub abuse, that at one stage he was known colloquially as Mr E. He was an expert witness at the inquest into the death of Leah Betts, who died after taking an Ecstasy tablet at her eighteenth birthday party in 1995.

John Henry was born at Greenwich, London on 11 March 1939, the eldest of four surviving children, Siobhan, Gabrielle, Michael. A fifth, Desmond, died in infancy in Charlestown during the Second World War. John attended St Joseph's Academy, Blackheath, London and went on to study medicine at King's College, London. As a twenty-year-old medical student he joined Opus Dei as a 'numerary member', committing himself to a life of celibacy.

In the 1960s while on holiday in Italy, John caught a throat infection

John Henry and Mrs Angela Henry.

which was inadequately treated and this lead to kidney failure. It was highly unlikely that he would live long as a dialysis patient and he gave up medicine for five years. The then head of Opus Dei, Mgr Josemaria Escrival, now St Josemaria, prayed fervently that a suitable kidney could be found for a transplant. In 1976, shortly after Escrival's death, a perfectly matching kidney was found and a successful operation gave John a new lease of life.

John Henry is survived in Charlestown by his aunt, Mrs Delia Henry, wife of the late Tony Henry, his cousins Cathal and John, and in the USA by his cousins, Tony Henry, Hilary Heaney and Mairead Salens, and in Portadown by Brian Henry.

May he rest in peace.

'DOWN MEMORY LANE'

Over to Ballaghaderreen I went,
The sports I went to view,
When the little horse jumped the fence,
And made them all subdue,
With Johnny Hanley on his back,
To encourage him along,
Amongst a cheering throng.

When the sport was over,
Down to Flannery's he did go,
He drank his wealth,
His horse's health,
Until his eyes did flow.
Then home he strode,
On his own home road,
The road he knew so well,
When nearing his home,
The cobb he nagged,
A story I have to tell.

Put more food stuff in my food box,
And I will jump that ditch,
Three times as quick,
For the sake of the rising dew,

So now my story ended,
I hope it pleases all,
Especially Johnny Hanley,
And his old Pye Ball.

Written by the late Johnny 'Sonny' Gallagher, Shoemaker, Cloonfane, Charlestown.